DEADLY BREW

She Loved Him to Death

By

T. F. Sisters

This book is a work of fiction. Names, characters, places, and incidents are products of the author's imagination or are used fictitiously. Any resemblance to actual events, locales, or persons, living or dead, is entirely coincidental.

© 1998, 2002 by T. F. Sisters. All rights reserved.

No part of this book may be reproduced, stored in a retrieval system, or transmitted by any means, electronic, mechanical, photocopying, recording, or otherwise, without written permission from the author.

ISBN: 0-7596-8660-2

Library of Congress Control Number: 2002090471

This book is printed on acid free paper.

Printed in the United States of America
Bloomington, IN

Cover Art By Kathie Bartel Doyal

1stBooks - rev. 04/25/02

Special thanks to the four sisters
without whom this book
would not have been possible

Elizabeth Roth Atwood
Viola Roth Ebert
Christene Roth Snider
Carol Roth Thomas

Thanks to Granny Irene Roth, our mother, for encouraging us to make something happen in our lives; to our father, Johann Maria Roth who gave us our sense of humor; to
Edward Joseph Roth for being our brother whom we love; to Rhett Murdaugh for his hours of typing; and to all those persons who gave us help, guidance and feedback:

Adrienne Ebert LeBlanc
Cecilé Gisele Ebert
Jonathan First
Wendy Roth
Bob Reiss
Jamie McDonnell
Kathie Bartel Doyal
Sherry Robertson Clement
Margaret Turnbow Quinn
Matthew Maisano
Bert Thomas
Shirley Dunn
Valerie Snow
Mary Mulrey
Barbara Heist

This book is dedicated to the love of my life who gave me my two greatest treasures and encouraged me to continue learning and never to say "It's too late."

Prologue

A violent shudder ripped through Samantha's body as she watched the casket being lifted from its resting place. "How could he have done this to me?" she thought resentfully. It was all his fault that she was having to go through this now. Samantha shuddered again and turned away. The last several years had been one long nightmare. First, Grant had left her for that miserable, home wrecking bitch. Then, he suddenly died before she had a chance to stop loving him. Not only did she have to suffer when he left her and her children; she had to suffer all over again when he died. He could have had the decency to wait until she didn't feel anything for him.

"You all right, Samantha?" Sgt. Martin's voice sounded far away. She dragged herself back from the abyss of her anger. "Yes, I'm okay, just tired, that's all. If he weren't already dead, I'd kill him for putting me and my children through this hell."

"Samantha, you know this is not really something he could have foreseen or prevented."

"He could have if he had been where he belonged. I'm sure she's responsible for this. She pushed him to it. I don't know how she did it, but I know she did."

"We'll soon know if there is any evidence to back up your suspicions, Samantha, but you have to prepare yourself for the possibility that the coroner may again conclude that it was simply a heart attack."

"It wasn't and you know it." Samantha retorted hotly. "Grant was a young, healthy man. He took good care of his body. I don't believe for one minute that he died of a sudden, unexpected heart attack. If he had a heart attack, that bitch caused it somehow."

Sgt. Martin studied the angry woman in front of him. The color was high on her cheeks and her eyes glittered. Her anger did not detract from her beauty. It only seemed to make her more magnetic. She was wearing an ivory pantsuit, which accentuated the creaminess of her skin in contrast to the thick, dark hair, which flowed loosely around her shoulders. Bob Martin could not conceive of a man walking away from her for another woman.

Samantha turned to look as the casket was placed into the coroner's vehicle, an ugly, white panel wagon with "County Coroner" emblazoned on the side in huge red letters. Sam Warfield, a friend and the county coroner, had made the trip out himself. He thought Samantha would feel better if he personally watched over Grant's remains. He didn't know what to say to her so he just gave her a quick nod and continued with the work at hand.

Samantha looked across the cemetery at the stiff, tight-lipped woman standing between two men. "You'll get yours now," she thought bitterly. "You almost got away with it." Samantha had battled long and hard to have Grant's body exhumed. The fact that a chance arrest of a local hoodlum had brought it about in no way lessened her feeling of victory.

Cynthia James was livid. She resented having to be here today, but her lawyers thought she should be for appearance sake. She berated herself for not insisting upon Grant's being cremated. What did they expect to accomplish by conducting an autopsy after all this time.
Cynthia had chosen to wear a soft blue pantsuit. She knew her eyes would appear bluer and her hair more golden. Even in these grim circumstances she couldn't resist dressing for the men in the group. Her lawyers had accompanied her to the cemetery and she had not been disappointed by their appreciative looks.
Cynthia glared across the grass at Samantha, Grant's first wife. This fiasco was all her doings. Cynthia wasn't sure how Samantha had persuaded a judge to order the exhumation, but nothing would come of it. They wouldn't find anything. What could they hope to find months after Grant's death. Samantha was simply harassing her. Grant's heart attack was certified by a respected physician who also happened to be Grant's friend.
Samantha's eyes swept once more over the bleak landscape that masqueraded as a last place of rest. It was one of those cemeteries that had been used by several generations. The old part of the cemetery had beautifully carved, albeit neglected gravestones. This front area was not so interesting. It was designed for low maintenance, and it was receiving none as far as Samantha could see. There were no upright grave markers, just little square stones on the ground with cheap brass urns sitting on top like rows and rows of little fat soldiers wearing helmets of fake flowers. The smell of freshly turned soil, which normally would have appealed to her senses, assailed her nostrils and made her feel nauseous. The angry hurt passed as quickly as it had come, and Samantha walked woodenly out of the Garden of Tranquility. Her feeling of victory was gone now. She didn't even notice Sgt. Martin's outstretched hand. She just felt very empty and hollow. The reality of Grant's death had suddenly hit her again just as hard as it had before.

Chapter 1

Stretching long and hard, Samantha glanced sleepily around the room. She noticed that Grant's briefcase was not on the desk. "I guess he's already gone or, perhaps, he didn't come home at all." Every now and then Grant had a case requiring that he keep very late hours. There had been several of those cases recently. Samantha sighed. She really thought that Grant spent too much time furthering his career, but she knew he had all their futures in mind.

Samantha looked around her comfortable bedroom and wished that she could snuggle under the warm covers for a while longer. Her bedroom had soft blue walls and carpet, which were accented by complimentary soft colors with just a splash of teal and coral on the champagne sofa. She always felt safe and calm in this room. It was truly her sanctuary. Sighing again audibly, she slid out of bed.

Samantha had awakened early as she did every morning to knock on Trey's door. She had to see that he ate a decent breakfast and wasn't tardy for school before she could dress herself. She missed Sadie's being here, but she was glad her daughter was doing so well her first year in college. Sadie was so excited about her classes; she hadn't missed a day.

Something terrible was about to happen. Every morning for a week now Samantha had been unable to shake this feeling of foreboding. Her intuitions were strong and generally correct. Her father had laughingly called her his little witch. Samantha's heart wrenched a little as she thought of her father. She still missed her parents. Usually, when she had these uneasy feelings, she knew exactly what was about to happen; but this time she just hadn't been able to identify it. She hated this vague, doomsday feeling. She knew that whatever was happening was going to affect her life profoundly, and she didn't think it would be positive.

Samantha finally ushered Trey out the door to school. Trey was big and mature looking for his age. Sometimes it was hard to remember he was young and not to expect him to behave like a mature man. It had been stressful this morning. He was sleepy and cranky. He had been especially slow. It was obvious that letting him stay up late was not a good idea. She wondered if he were in some difficulty at school or perhaps had not done his homework. She and Grant had to constantly issue reminders about keeping his grades up.

Samantha stared blankly into her closet as she thought about her son. She reached into the closet and absently flipped through the neatly hung clothing. Samantha always hung complete outfits. Since she didn't have to waste time matching her clothing, she could spend a few more minutes with Trey in the mornings. Once in awhile Grant would have breakfast at home, but most times he simply had a doughnut at the office. Samantha decided on a chocolate brown linen pantsuit fitted at the waist with a wide belt. Her new ivory silk blouse was a nice contrast to the brown linen. She applied makeup sparingly, dressed quickly, and added small gold hoops to her ears. She looked in the mirror approvingly and picked up her purse. Samantha's mother had taught her to carry what she called a universal purse, one that she didn't have to change with every outfit. Samantha was very grateful for that lesson this morning as she hurried down the stairs.

As Samantha started to the front door, she saw Grant's topcoat lying on the sofa. He obviously had been home sometime during the night. "Why didn't he awaken me," she thought with mild irritation. "And when is he going to learn to hang up his coat." She picked it up annoyed at his thoughtlessness. Didn't he realize that she worked, too? She didn't have time to pick up after him. Trey made enough work for her.

On the front was a huge spot of something reddish-brown looking. Samantha looked more closely. It looked almost like lipstick. Samantha looked again. It really did look like lipstick. She shook her head, disgusted with herself for even thinking such a thing. If this were anyone but Grant, she would be suspicious, but he was much too involved in his work to have time for another woman. He obviously had been eating those disgustingly messy tacos he loved so much. She would never understand why he insisted upon eating at that greasy spoon taco joint when, otherwise, he took such care of himself. Fortunately, he didn't indulge in tacos very often, because when he did he really overdid it. "I guess I'd better have it cleaned," she thought. "He'll need it now that the weather is turning colder."

Samantha looked once more at the dark red smudge. She spoke aloud now. "Grant has always been faithful to a fault." As a matter of fact, she recalled that the joke among their male friends was "if you want a fun boys' night out you don't invite Grant."

Samantha had heard the joke and had taken secret pride in it.

Samantha began to empty the pockets. She pulled out a matchbook. Grant didn't smoke. Why would he be carrying matches? She looked at the inscription, "Rose's." Rose's was a nightclub over in Talulah. Why had he been there? "Maybe he was there with a client," she thought. He did have a few "unusual" clients. Samantha chuckled as she recalled a couple of those clients. There was the lady with the purple hair and the big shopping bag that kept catching items, which fell off the counter as she walked by. Her family was quite prominent in another city, and they kept Grant on retainer just to bail her out and reimburse merchants. Grant could have assigned this work to an associate, but he genuinely like the woman and her family and enjoyed keeping her out of trouble.

Once a year Grant gave a big barbeque at his house for all the law enforcement officers. In return, when "Mrs. Purple Hair" made a mistake, they called him.

Samantha laughed out loud as she remembered the man with the plaid patchwork pants and tuxedo jacket. She had asked Grant why he was arrested only to be told he was not a criminal. Rather he was very wealthy and very eccentric. They were estate planning. "Oh, well, as they say, don't judge a book by its cover," Samantha thought ruefully as she checked her watch. She was going to be late. Samantha despised tardiness in her and in others.

Chapter 2

Roderick stared across the room at Cynthia, his beautiful young wife, curled up on the sofa reading. She appeared so content. He was not a stupid man, he knew his money had played a huge role in her decision to marry him. He didn't mind. He enjoyed having a gorgeous, young woman around. She loved traveling as much as he did. She threw herself boldly and enthusiastically into each new adventure. It made him feel young to be with her. She was provocative, clever, and totally uninhibited in bed. Well aware of the play on phonetics, he had given her the pet name "Sin." He always teased her saying that what she did to him was downright sinful. It was their private joke. Her expertise made him perform as well as any man half his age. His money may have enticed her, but she was not disappointing him. They had been married about three years and had a comfortable relationship. Roderick had retired when he married her so they could travel around the world.

Roderick had initially made a fortune in pharmaceuticals. Over the years he had diversified his investments to include several high tech ventures. He still remembered those twelve-hour days, six days a week. It had been an exhausting pace, but he had been a young buck then and thought he was immortal. Now he had top-notch managers, so his business affairs were in good hands. His only regret was that he had no children to follow in his footsteps. He had given up hope even though Cynthia was still of childbearing age. Now it was too late. Dr. Levinson had told him yesterday that his days were numbered. All tests indicated that he had an inoperable brain tumor. "Brain tumors are unpredictable," Jim had said. "It could be a week or it could be a year."

Roderick knew he was still an attractive man, tall and lean. He tried to stay in shape because of a little heart problem a few years ago. He needed plenty of exercise, so he played golf several times a week and racquetball two nights a week. Since he ate sensibly and avoided excess fat in his diet, he maintained his weight at a consistent level. His thick, white hair was a startling contrast to his dark tan and twinkling, blue eyes. He had lived a good life, so age had been very kind to him. Now, however, he faced rapid deterioration. He hated for Cynthia to see him waste away. He knew she didn't love him the way he loved her, but she seemed genuinely fond of him and he had been able to amuse her. He dreaded telling her the truth. He needed to set his affairs in order immediately. He wanted to make sure she was protected financially for the rest of her life.

Madeline Tullis had been praising that young attorney she was using. "Maybe, I'll work with him," Roderick thought. "Damned if I'll listen to a lecture from Frank Harrelson about leaving everything to Cynthia." Roderick hated not knowing how rapidly the tumors would progress. He believed in controlling his future, but he had no future. Roderick felt mildly bitter and a little sad. He was enjoying his life with Cynthia more than he had ever enjoyed anyone. "Maybe it's better this way before she decides one day that I'm too old for her." Roderick knew for sure he couldn't survive her walking out on him.

Cynthia laid her novel aside. It had been a quiet evening at home. They had just returned from Greece. It had been a good trip. Roderick had done everything possible to show her a great time, but it still lacked excitement. He was so good and generous to her. He had purchased expensive jewelry for her from each country they visited. She knew Roderick loved her very much. She felt a small pang of guilt because she could not return his feelings. She believed that Roderick never suspected her lack of real passion for him. She had played her role of loving wife and passionate lover extremely well. She found him a very attractive man despite his being slightly boring. His money bought the luxuries she craved and this made him infinitely more interesting.

Nevertheless, Cynthia wished Roderick were a young, virile man who could make her burn with desire. She had a need for danger and intrigue. She had always enjoyed living on the edge. The power to make men senseless with desire for her was a huge turn on. To this end she bought expensive clothes with a subtle, seductive allure, some less subtle than others. She knew she had beautiful breasts and a figure that turned heads. She had recognized her power over men at an early age and had used it to leave poverty and boredom behind. She knew men would forget where she came from if she made them feel macho and important. She had learned to project a vulnerability that brought out the protective urges in men. She knew Roderick felt that way even when he was teasingly telling her how sinful she was.

Smiling, Cynthia glanced at Roderick. He was exceptionally quiet tonight. She wondered if something was bothering him. She had caught him staring into space on several occasions. She wondered if his heart was giving him trouble. She knew he had taken his medication faithfully. However, he had cut their recent trip short to come home. He had insisted that a pressing business situation needed his immediate attention. He had left the house early yesterday and had not returned until after dinner. She hoped there were no serious problems with his business. He always discussed personal problems with her, but he didn't like to worry her with business. Since he had not confided in her, she assumed there was something awry at the office. "Maybe I'll lure him to bed. That always lifts his spirits," Cynthia thought.

"You're very quiet tonight, Roderick. Is anything wrong?"

He looked at her and debated telling her. He decided to wait. "No, just thinking about some estate planning."

"I thought you'd done all that," Cynthia remarked.

"Well, you know inheritance laws are constantly changing. If anything should happen to me, I wouldn't want you to have any problems."

"Nothing's going to happen to you, Roderick; you're in good health," Cynthia exclaimed.

Roderick mentally winced. "How am I going to tell her?" He wondered. "I don't want to worry her, but it's inevitable."

Cynthia stood up, stretched in her catlike fashion and crossed to Roderick. "Why don't we go upstairs, dear, we haven't properly celebrated our return home," she said, smiling seductively. She bent over and teased his lips lightly with her tongue. Without another word Roderick rose and followed her. "We can talk tomorrow," he thought.

Chapter 3

Grant leaned back in his chair and reviewed his day. It had been a bad one. It wasn't enough that his financial peccadilloes had caught up with him, but he had also been soundly trounced and humiliated in court. He should have won that case hands down. It had been his rotten luck to draw Judge Henry who hated him and always ruled against him.

Grant smiled as he remembered the reason for Judge Henry's wrath, however. The prize had been worth it. Before Grant or Parker Henry had been married, they had been rivals for Penelope Winslow. Grant had enjoyed some of the hottest, most turbulent sex of his life with Penelope, and he had not hesitated to let Parker know it. How was he to know old Parker would marry her? Penelope had really wanted to marry Grant, but he saw no reason for that since she was already providing everything he wanted from her. "No need to buy the cow if you can get the milk through the fence," his father always said. Grant had no doubt he could still do that and he toyed briefly with the idea.

As a matter of fact, Grant wasn't too sure Penelope's first child was not his. Missy had been born a close nine months after the wedding. Grant remembered his private little bachelorette party for Penelope. They hadn't let anything inhibit their spontaneity. Missy did have red hair and blue eyes just like him. Penelope and Parker both had dark hair and eyes.

Grant was a big, good-looking guy with an abundance of sandy red hair, which he kept trimmed short in an effort to keep it under control. Grant had been a football star in high school. He strived to keep his body in top athletic condition. Penelope had been determined to explore that body thoroughly one more time before her marriage, and Grant, still single, had been only too happy to oblige her.

Grant wallowed a little longer in thoughts of a torrid turn in the bed of Penelope Henry, before he jerked back to reality and the true cause of his frustration. It wasn't Judge Henry or the Styles case. It was money. He needed money badly. He had made some speculative investments in penny stocks and junk bonds, and the market had gone south on him. Grant had good information, insider information. He couldn't miss, so he had invested heavily. "So much for insider information," he thought bitterly. How in the hell was he going to tell Samantha that Sadie would not be able to continue the College of Wooster as they had planned. Real shame, too. It was rated one of the best private colleges in the nation. It had a ratio of one professor for every eleven and one-half students. Grant had attended school there as had his father before him.

The College of Wooster was a small college enrolling about seventeen hundred fifty students. The campus was situated in the quiet little town of

Wooster, Ohio. Tree lined streets and older, well-kept homes added to its quaintness and charm. The school itself was modern, well equipped, and well staffed. They had recently added a dormitory consisting of well-designed suites and the beautiful new Ebert Fine Arts Building. The original buildings on campus had been renovated and were well maintained.

Sadie would be heartbroken. Grant's heart felt heavy as he imagined her face when they told her. He felt even more depressed when he thought of his father. His parents weren't wealthy, but they had scrimped and saved to help him go to Wooster when he had received a scholarship for his tuition. His father had attended on a scholarship, as well, but he had been forced to work to pay the additional expenses. Forest came from a fine, old family whom no longer had great wealth, but still managed to present a well-bred and cultured façade. The James family had owned a chain of quality furniture stores throughout the state. Due to the advent of huge, wholesale warehouses, they had been forced to downscale their operations, but they still maintained a comfortable living standard.

Grant felt badly. He knew that his father would insist on trying to send Sadie to Wooster anyway. It would be a lot more expensive now and Sadie didn't have a scholarship. She was smart enough, but she just had not applied herself. Grant had to admit he had not pushed her. She was such a sweet, generous, lovable girl. She could always talk him into relaxing any role.

Grant slowly picked up the phone. He needed to call George Nabors. George was a good friend and also the president of the local bank. Grant did all his business with Brookston, a community bank that he had helped to organize. He and a group of friends, such as George, had become tired of dealing with big banks and had decided to found a small community bank which would direct itself to the interests and needs of the local community. Grant had invested heavily. Thank God, for this was one investment that had been successful. If he could sell his stock, maybe he could crawl over the financial hump. There was just one problem. The stock was privately traded and could not be sold to an outsider without unanimous approval of the other investors. He was hoping George would pick up a few thousand shares.

"George, how are you? Did you play today?" Wednesday was usually George's golf day. Grant laughed, "How much did you take from him? I can hear him now grumbling like it was his last dollar."

"How is Sally these days? I don't know how she puts up with Sam and his dour personality."

"George, I've decided to diversify my investments, and I'm thinking of letting go of some of my Brookston stock. Are you interested in picking up a few thousand shares?" There was a long silence. Then, "I have another major opportunity and I need some quick cash, George, otherwise I'd never consider releasing any of my Brookston stock."

"Yes, I know it will dilute my position, but this other opportunity is too hot to pass up."

"No, I don't think you'd have interest in it, George." Another pause, "Well, it's being very closely held. I'll ask, but I doubt they'll admit anyone else."

"Well, think about my offer, George. If you're not interested maybe someone else will be."

"No, I won't offer it to anyone else until I hear from you."

Grant heard a sound. He swung around and saw his mother standing in front of his desk. "George, I'll ring you tomorrow. My mother has just come in."

"Yes, I will." Grant dropped the phone in its cradle.

"That was George Nabors, Mother, he sends his regards. What are you doing here?"

Margaret beamed at her son. "I was shopping at Beeman's just around the corner and thought it would be nice to have a cup of coffee with you." Margaret's forehead creased and she gave her son a long questioning look. "I detected a troubled note in your voice. Is something wrong between you and George?"

Grant shook his head, relieved that she hadn't heard anything. Just at that moment Margaret spoke again.

"I couldn't help overhearing your conversation, dear, what is this new opportunity. It must be something really big for you to sell your Brookston stock. That's your baby, and you've been very happy about its success."

Grant looked at his mother. His heart fell. She was the one person on earth to whom he had never been able to lie. He knew he couldn't do it now. In a way, he was relieved. He welcomed her knowing. She had a talent for making things look brighter.

His mother was still a very attractive woman, tall and elegant. Even though she was getting up there in years, she had a much younger appearance. As her hair had greyed she had kept a soft blond rinse on it. Her blue gray eyes always held a twinkle. His mother was strong and had a very positive attitude about everything. He was sure that her positive approach to life had kept her young. He admired his mother very much. They had a special bond.

"There is no opportunity, Mom." Grant replied hesitantly.

"But, I heard you tell George you had this great opportunity." Margaret exclaimed.

"I told him that because I didn't want him to know the real reason for selling."

"What is the reason?" Margaret asked, anxiety showing on her face. She knew it must be serious if Grant was willing to part with his Brookston stock. She could see in his face the reluctance to tell her.

"I've made some bad investments," Grant blurted out. "I've gotten behind on my payments on both houses." In addition to their house in the city, Grant and Samantha had a nice three-bedroom cottage in the country. They spent most of their summers there away from the sweltering heat of the city.

"Oh, honey, maybe Dad and I can help you."

Grant looked at her lovingly for several seconds. He and his mother had a wonderful relationship. She was always there for him, supportive and never judgmental. "I don't think so, Mother," using the formal address, Grant said slowly, "I'm afraid the problem is beyond a few thousand dollars."

"Oh, my goodness, Grant," shock showed on Margaret's now worried brow, "How much beyond?"

"Several hundred thousand." Margaret was visibly shaken. She had thought maybe ten, even twenty thousand, but not several hundred thousand. She felt her stomach lurch. This was not something she could kiss and make go away.

Grant came to his mother. He could see she was very upset. "I'm sorry, I didn't mean to upset you, Mom. I'll see you home, but please don't tell Dad just yet. I shouldn't have told you. I should have worked it out on my own."

"No, no, Grant, just a cup of coffee and I'll be okay."

Grant's secretary had long since gone home, and he had no idea how to make coffee in the machine here at the office. "There's a little coffee shop at the corner. I think they are still open." As they walked down the stairs, Margaret's mind was rapidly turning over ways that she and Dad could help Grant and his dear family. She truly loved Samantha and their two wonderful grandchildren, Sadie and Trey.

Grant had worked hard building his firm. For several years he had practiced alone, but it had reached the point that he was turning business away because he couldn't keep up. About five years ago he had invited two young attorneys to join him. They had not disappointed him and they had since been made partners. One specialized in litigation while the other dealt in securities. Grant devoted most of his time now to estate planning, trusts and related matters. James, Dunn & McDaniels were highly respected. Grant was very proud of their accomplishments, but now he was very worried. He had jeopardized his own financial future and maybe that of his firm.

Chapter 4

As Grant prepared for his appointment with Cynthia Barker, he remembered the first time he had met Mr. and Mrs. Roderick Barker. Mrs. Lawrence Tullis, widow of the oil magnate and founder of L.J.T. Oil Properties, Inc., had referred them to him. They said he had come highly recommended. Grant thought ruefully, "I guess so considering the hours I have devoted to the sizable estate of L.J. Tullis and its distribution, and the fact that Mrs. Tullis questions every minute of my time trying to shave off a few dollars from my fee." Well, she apparently acknowledged his worth if she had given his name to the Barkers.

Roderick was a nice enough fellow of sixty. He was intelligent, personable, and obviously a financial wizard. His wife, Cynthia, was approximately thirty-five years old, give or take two or three years. Her age had not been mentioned, but Grant was usually pretty accurate in his judgment of age and character. One thing for sure, she was one of the most beautiful women he had ever met. She had a sophisticated elegance, which belied the sexual magnetism she radiated. Grant had quickly and appreciatively reviewed her petite body, thick mane of pale blonde hair, firm full breasts, long legs, and full, perfectly shaped lips. She had a dazzling smile that seemed to light up the room. He had heard Roderick call her "Sin." Grant had to smile at the implication. She certainly brought sinful thoughts to his mind. As a matter of fact, the effect she had on him made him uncomfortable. She had become almost an obsession. She crept into his thoughts constantly.

Roderick had been very specific with his requests that day, detailing exactly what he expected of Grant. Grant remembered how startled he had been when Roderick had looked him in the eye and said, "I'll soon be a dead man. I have an inoperable brain tumor. It is questionable how long I will be mentally competent. I want my affairs in order before I deteriorate. I want to be sure that Cynthia is protected. She is to be the beneficiary of my entire estate with the exception of only a few small bequests." Roderick made it clear that, although he had a previous marriage, it had been settled satisfactorily and this would not be a factor at probate time. He further advised that he had no legitimate or illegitimate children. He had then handed Grant a list of small bequests to his brother, ex-wife, long time employees, and several children of friends. Grant had admired his calm approach to everything. He wasn't sure he could be as courageous in the same circumstances.

Grant felt a sense of excitement as Cynthia was shown into his office. She was wearing a snugly fitted, basic black dress with a neckline scooped just low enough to show a hint of cleavage. A pair of high heel, strap sandals revealed very shapely ankles. "How could such simplicity be so stunning," he thought.

As he rose to shake her hand, he said, "Mrs. Barker, you are looking well considering the circumstances. How is Roderick?"

Cynthia smiled demurely as she took his hand. She liked this tall, auburn-haired man with the devil-may-care smile. His blue eyes looked directly into hers as he spoke. He inspired trust. He also excited her making her wish for a speedy end to Roderick's illness.

Feeling ashamed of her thoughts, she responded, "He's not doing well at all. He's still mentally alert, but his physical condition has worsened." Again flashing a helpless little me smile, she released Grant's hand.

"Mrs. Barker, what can I do for you today?"

"Please, call me Cynthia. Mrs. always sounds so formal." Her deep throaty voice sent a thrill through him.

"Sure, whatever you prefer." He felt like a schoolboy falling over his words. How could a mere voice rattle him so much?

"Grant, you don't mind my calling you that, do you? After all, we will be working very closely on my husband's affairs." The word "affair" sent a tingling sensation through Grant.

"I've prepared a draft of Roderick's assets. You need to review it with his financial people to be sure it is complete. The will has already been signed, but it would be better if he signed the list of assets, as well, while he is still mentally competent."

"What difference does it make if he is mentally competent?" Cynthia had a perplexed expression. "I'm his wife."

"Roderick has left everything to you, but I just want to eliminate any potential complications. We may need a small codicil to head off any contest of the will. Has he ever been married before, any brothers or sisters, parents living?"

"Well, yes, he has a brother and was married once before. What difference does that make?"

"Well, I want to make sure that no one else has a claim to the estate. Did he have any children from his prior marriage?"

"No, there were no children."

"Most of Roderick's assets were acquired prior to your marriage, weren't they?"

"Yes, of course, I wouldn't have…have…" catching herself, "wouldn't have thought that mattered." She was a bit shaken. She certainly didn't want Grant thinking she was a gold digger and would not have married Roderick if he had not been wealthy.

Grant continued with his probing questions. Explaining the implications of each situation as it related to probate law.

After Cynthia left, Grant considered their conversation. He hadn't needed to reaffirm all the relationships, but he had wanted to prolong the visit. Roderick had covered all the specifics in their first visit. Roderick had no children from his marriage of thirty-five years to Estella. They had divorced six months prior to Roderick's marriage to Cynthia. There should be no problems from Estella. She had received a huge property settlement. The present mansion had been built after Cynthia and Roderick married and was set up as joint tenants entitling each to one half of the value in the event of a divorce. Roderick had specified joint tenants with right of survivorship to protect Cynthia's deed to the property. He directed that the will be written with a no contest clause, a small legacy to his brother, Randolph, and additional bequests to his former wife, Estella, several employees, and three children of friends. Grant was one of the best. His expertise in probate law was no secret. He anticipated no problems with the execution of the estate. All things considered, Cynthia would be a very wealthy woman upon the death of Roderick. Grant speculated on how nice it would be to have no financial problems. He felt guilty that his forays into the junk bond field had put him and Samantha in a less than comfortable financial position.

Chapter 5

Cynthia felt depressed. She wasn't very good at playing nursemaid. She had hired private duty nurses to assist, but she still had to be present frequently for appearance sake. She had never been able to be around sickness or death. Roderick's condition had worsened rapidly in the last few weeks. Cynthia was nervous about his impending death and the consequences to her and his estate. She knew she wasn't capable of making business decisions especially for Roderick's diverse business interests. Early in their marriage Roderick had tried to talk to her about his business affairs, but she was only interested in the financial returns, which supported her life style and designer shopping sprees. She hadn't anticipated his current, serious health problem. She often joked with her friends that all she knew about a dollar was that it was green and kept her happy. No, she couldn't take Roderick's failing health lightly, it scared her. She was worried about his business empire. Although he had first-rate executives managing his businesses and an incredible stockbroker, who had masterminded many of his best investments, there were still many decisions that had to be made by Roderick, himself.

"Grant James seems to be an extremely intelligent man with excellent insight concerning the financial world, maybe he could advise me. I'll give him a call tomorrow."

"Besides," Cynthia thought amusedly, "he's not hard on the eyes either." She suppressed a wicked smile and made a note to call him early in the morning.

~ ~ ~ ~ ~ ~ ~ ~ ~ ~ ~ ~ ~ ~ ~ ~

As Grant finished his first cup of coffee, Della buzzed, "Mr. James, I have Mrs. Barker on the line."

"I'll take it. Thank you, Della." He took a deep breath and slowly exhaled to stifle the quiver he felt in his throat. Lord, why did this woman affect him like this? He was a happily married man with two children not some randy, young stud. Yet the excitement he felt each time he talked to her, much less saw her, was amazing. "How can I help you, Cynthia?"

"I just wanted to confirm that all of Roderick's affairs are in order. He seems to be failing fast. I believe the end is near."

He felt an immediate physical response to her husky voice. He was embarrassed, but proud that the "old boy" could still give a healthy salute to a lovely lady. He cleared his throat and asked, "Would you like to discuss these matters in person, or can I answer your questions over the phone?"

Cynthia had actually been hoping for a reason to see Grant. He was vibrant and alive. She was sick of the smell that accompanied death. Why did it have to be so gruesome? Seeing the chance to escape the dreary depths of her prison, she seized the opportunity. With sickness hanging over her lovely estate it had become almost unbearable. Roderick had been so virile, so dashing when she met him. Of course, his money may have clouded her vision a tiny bit. "Right! Cynthia, give it a break. You know his money was the major attraction. I wonder if Grant James is wealthy?" she mused. Realizing she had not answered Grant's question, she replied, "I'd really like to come to your office unless, of course, you could get away for a drink at Rose's. It's about halfway between my home and your office." Cynthia chose a club where she occasionally had met friends from her past. A place where they were not likely to see any of Roderick's friends.

Knowing he should insist upon a meeting at his office or at least a very public restaurant, he wavered. Taking a deep breath, "Well...if that is easier for you. I'm sure you do not want to be away from Roderick very long." Grant cursed himself for his weakness.

Not wanting to appear too callous and uncaring, she replied, "Oh, you're very considerate, I don't think I should be away for very long."

Chapter 6

Samantha stared out at the bleak, winter day. She felt the chill in her bones. She had tried everything to feel warm but nothing seemed to help. She hated cold weather. She found it depressing and uncomfortable. Her day had been strange. She found it difficult to concentrate and nostalgia seemed to overwhelm her. Several times she had caught herself going down memory lane. It wasn't that she was unhappy with her life, she just had this vague feeling of discontent. Recently Grant had begun working such long hours, and with Sadie away at school and Trey wrapped up in his own activities, sometimes she felt very alone. She didn't know what had triggered her reflective mood. Maybe it had been her new client, Peter Stanton. She still remembered how her heart had raced at the sight of him. She hoped he didn't notice her shortness of breath. She was sure her face was flushed. Hopefully, he thought it was the result of the brisk wind. After all, it was the first winter chill. It had been a long time since she had felt that attracted to another man. Remembering, she was embarrassed at how her body responded to him; but, my gosh, what woman wouldn't respond. He was ruggedly handsome, tall and lean, and moved with the grace of a panther. It was obvious he spent a lot of time outdoors. The combination of dark tan, amber eyes and that lopsided grin that revealed dazzling white teeth was breathtaking. She felt as giddy as a teenager.

Pulling herself back from what she instinctively knew was dangerous territory, Samantha turned her thoughts to her children. Sadie had grown into a beautiful girl. She had gotten her height from her Grandmother James. She had clear blue eyes that seemed to look into your soul. With her thick, auburn hair and long legs, she easily could have been a model, but Sadie wasn't interested in the glamour world. She was a caregiver, and wanted to work in that field. Maybe that was the most beautiful part of her. She was kind and unpretentious. She planned to work with children with special needs. She would make a great teacher.

Samantha felt a surge of pride. She loved her daughter very much. She liked the person Sadie had become. She knew it was going to be expensive to keep her in Wooster, but Sadie deserved to go to the school of her choice. "Besides," Samantha thought, "Grant and I have invested carefully, so money is not a problem." After all, Sadie's father and grandfather had gone there. Samantha knew Sadie could have earned a scholarship if she had studied harder, but it had been her choice to devote a large amount of time to the Special Olympics. Samantha couldn't fault her for that. She preferred for her daughter to care deeply about the lives of people rather than make straight A's. She knew Grant felt differently, but then Sadie tended to work at pleasing her mother.

Samantha's thoughts drifted to Trey. She knew Grant was upset about his grades. Trey just didn't apply himself. His grades could have been far above average. She knew in her heart that he could do anything to which he set his mind. She had observed him recently when he helped her with the fundraiser for the Heritage Museum. He had a sharp mind for details and figures. He really kept things moving. She had never realized how organized he could be. He was a real charmer, too. Everyone loved him, especially the elderly ladies. He had them eating out of his hand and opening their checkbooks. She was sure his participation had made the project much more successful than she had anticipated. Samantha unconsciously smiled. If he could do that at eighteen years, just think how dynamic he would be when he matured.

Trey was tall like Sadie; however, that was where the resemblance ended. He had blond hair and his twinkling, brown eyes crinkled with engaging creases when he laughed. He laughed a lot. He had always been happy. Even as a baby, he rarely cried. Trey moved like the wind. Samantha guessed that was why he was doing so well in basketball. The coach said he had the makings of a star athlete if he would stay focused. What Samantha liked most about Trey was that he wasn't afraid to show affection. She could remember many times as a child when he would dash in the house and yell, "Mom, I love you," and out the back door he'd go to join his friends. Even now, he would hug her and kiss her cheek spontaneously. Samantha was proud of her children. They had heart.

Samantha's thoughts turned to her husband, Grant; he used to be thoughtful and romantic. She couldn't remember when things had changed. Recently Grant had begun working long hours, too many hours to leave time for his family. She knew his job was demanding, but she missed the old times. Samantha smiled as she remembered how it had been when they were first married. She'd leave work at Big Al's Restaurant when they were in college, open her car door and find a handwritten note from Grant, "Thinking of you. I love you. G." Sometimes, he'd leave a single paper rose on her pillow. They couldn't afford the real thing then. On special occasions, he always bought that perfect gift, never forgot their anniversary, and always shopped early for Christmas. Sighing she thought, "There's always a price to pay for success."

Grant had always been a faithful husband and a great father. Even as the children grew up, he was their friend and confidante. He never missed Sadie's dance recitals or Trey's soccer games. Grant encouraged them to be involved in extracurricular activities. He wanted Trey to be an athlete as he had been. Grant had been a star football player in high school and college. He might have gone pro if his shoulder hadn't started giving him so much trouble. Grant was proud of his physique. He still kept in shape and was as lean and broad shouldered as any young athlete. Samantha was acutely aware of other women's admiring glances.

"He is still a handsome man," Samantha thought smugly, "although a little too serious of late. When did we begin to drift apart?" Samantha realized she couldn't answer that question. They had always been very close, but they rarely spent time together anymore. She limited the amount of clients she accepted for her design business; however, she was very involved in the community. She did that mostly for Grant. She knew her participation was important for his career. A leading attorney in town had an image to uphold. She was on the board for the Arts and Humanities Council, President of Business and Professional Women, Director of the Tourism Committee at the Chamber of Commerce, plus she was an active fundraiser for several of the charities in town. Grant was proud of her status in the community. She liked making him proud, but there were times when she would have liked just to be herself. It would be nice to do things spontaneously without living on a schedule, just to enjoy life.

Chapter 7

Grant was nervous, chain smoking, and clicking his pen against the glass top of his desk. They had come so close last time they had dinner at Simm's landing. The piano bar and cocktails before dinner, a lovely Chardonnay with the meal, and a snifter of Courvoisier after dinner set the stage for what followed in the parking lot. Grant was embarrassed as he replayed the scene in his head. He acted like an adolescent; groping and grunting in the front seat of the car complete with steamed up windows. His behavior had been juvenile. It was wrong and terribly irresponsible of him. What would Samantha or the kids think if they knew? "Even worse," he thought in horror, "what if one of my clients or associates had seen me?" He knew that one or two local attorneys conducted business outside their offices.

He suddenly saw the image of Samantha the day they met. He was in the Student Union when she walked in. She was so mature and sophisticated, every inch a lady. She was graceful and beautiful. All the girls around her looked clumsy by comparison. He hadn't been able to take his eyes off her. She looked up and their eyes locked. For him, it was love at first sight. Luckily, she felt the same way. They had been a couple ever since. He remembered all the concerts they attended. Fleetwood Mac had been one of their favorites. They had claimed "Love Song" as their own. That first rush had cooled, but they still had a very comfortable relationship and two wonderful children.

Grant felt guilty. How could he jeopardize everything they had built together? "No, I can't let this go any further. I should withdraw from this case, but I need the fee. Damn my financial problems. Damn it all. Damn the whole situation." Grant groaned and let out an audible sigh. Cynthia had tasted so good, and the soft, hot skin between her legs felt fantastic. "I can't walk away. I want her more than any woman I've ever known."

Grant pulled himself back to the present wearing the face of a tormented man. "I've got to focus," Grant told himself. "I have work to do. I've got to concentrate. My finances are a disaster. I should be working twice as hard to bring in extra money and I'm a wreck. I'm short tempered with my associates. I've got to get a grip."

Chapter 8

"Mr. James, Mrs. Barker is here to see you."

"Thank you, Della. Show her in, then you can leave for the day. I'll close up for you."

"Oh, thank you, Mr. James, I need to pick up my new dress from the alterations lady before five-thirty."

Grant felt his pulse quicken as Cynthia walked into his office and closed the door. Their eyes met as he clicked the lock. Unspoken consent was electric between them. Their passion could not be denied any longer. She stepped seductively out of her heels as she loosened his tie. She reached back to unzip her dress as he tossed his shirt to the side. They came together in an embrace; her dress slithered to the floor. His mouth devoured hers. He grasped her lacy bra and felt her nipples under his touch.

Grant flipped the snap on the front of her bra and eased it off her shoulders, as he caressed her neck and breast with his lips and tongue. Removing her hands from his neck she released his belt and with experienced fingers quickly unzipped his slacks. Sliding them down his body, she began to explore. Grant felt her tongue as she caressed his throbbing member. He gasped as he felt the pressure of her lips and the hot pleasure she gave him. He gently pulled her up and kissed her hard on the mouth. Sliding her slip off her hips, he discovered a black garter belt and no panties to slow his progress. He sank to his knees lowering her to the thick carpet. He slowly moved down her body, thrilling at the firmness of her voluptuous breasts and savoring the taste of her forbidden fruit. She moaned as he spread her legs and gently massaged her with his tongue and finger. She gasped as Grant covered her body and plunged his full length into her. She came quickly. "Oh! Oh! Oh! Please, Grant, harder, faster. Yes! Yes! Ahhh...um!" A moan of total release escaped her lips. It was so great to be with a young, virile man.

Although Grant had not yet climaxed, she was already planning the next act. She never liked one act plays. Much too boring for her taste. It was like a game of cat and mouse with the spoils of the kill at the end. "He's mine." She thought smugly. "It's just a matter of time." She would not be alone when Roderick died. "Samantha, sugar, your days are numbered. What I want, I get!"

Cynthia was not sure she had ever been taken in such total bliss and abandon as tonight. As Grant took her for the third time that night, she was certain of her catch. How fortunate...rich, good looking, and an incredible lover. She had missed the power, the heat, and the pure sex of a younger, more virile man. Anticipation of clandestine meetings, quickies in the elevator, or a power punch on his desk or office sofa created the intrigue she needed. She had always enjoyed creative lovemaking. It kept the temperature high.

Before leaving Grant's office they made plans to meet there again on Thursday after Della left for the day. His law partners were always gone before he and Della left. Grant didn't want anyone to get suspicious. He knew he couldn't give Cynthia up, not after tonight. He and Cynthia had agreed it wasn't a good idea to be seen out in public places too frequently.

~~~~~~~~~~~~~~~~

Grant woke with a start. "Oh my God, Cynthia, it's four a.m. I've got to get home, shower and get back to town for a breakfast meeting." He wasn't surprised they had fallen asleep. They had made love until they were both exhausted. They couldn't seem to get enough of one another. Grant tensed as he realized how reckless they had become. They must be more careful in the future.

Cynthia and Grant dressed quickly, tidied the office, hurriedly locked up, and dashed for their cars. "How could I have been so careless." Grant chastised himself. "Damn stupid, falling asleep naked on the office floor! Boy, Della would have had cardiac arrest at her usual seven-thirty a.m. arrival." Grant silently thanked Burlington Northern for that four a.m. train. If not for its whistle, they might still be asleep. Grant chuckled to himself imagining the look on Della's face had they not awakened. His thoughts turned to Cynthia. When Roderick died she would become a very wealthy woman. How tempting she was...sexy...beautiful, rich, and insatiable. She couldn't get enough of his attention. He wondered...she could be the answer to his financial problems.

As Cynthia eased the Mercedes up the long drive to the palatial estate she and Roderick called home, she was startled to see several lights on in the house and Dr. Levinson's car by the entrance.

"Oh, damn, damn," she said as she flicked the interior light on and quickly added some lipstick and ran a brush through her hair. "That's just great. Roderick must have taken a turn for the worse. What do I tell everyone? 'Oh, I've been humping Roderick's attorney in his office, on his desk, on his floor...don't forget the couch.' Oh, Roderick, I'm sorry, you knew I'd never make a very good wife or for that matter be faithful."

Taking a deep breath to compose herself, she quickly entered the house and was met by Mildred, Roderick's long time maid. "Mildred, what's happened, has Roderick taken a bad turn? Is everything okay?"

Mildred gave her a withering look. "No, Mrs. Barker, all is not well. Mr. Roderick passed away about an hour ago." Although Mildred didn't approve of some of Cynthia's actions in recent weeks, she had to admit that the last four years of Mr. Roderick's life had been blissfully happy with Mrs. Barker. She reminded herself that Mrs. Barker was still young and vibrant. Who was she to be judge and jury? Still, it was hard for Mildred to forgive her absence. Mr. Roderick had called for her several times before he went.

Cynthia stifled a sob and clamped her hand over her mouth. She hadn't expected this reaction. Was it her guilt? No, Roderick had been kind and extremely generous with her. His classic good looks, his elegant bearing, and the electric atmosphere that always seemed to surround him had been a powerful tonic for her. He always made her feel like royalty. She had to admit that while most younger men looked at her with only lust in their eyes, Roderick's eyes always elevated her to a place of honor. He saw her as a fragile piece of rare porcelain, as Faberge`, a crown jewel in his eyes. "Yes, I guess, I am feeling much like a traitor at this moment." Cynthia ran upstairs to the bedroom. She couldn't believe it. Roderick had been fine when she left. She hesitated then she walked slowly to the bed. Cynthia apologized to the empty, lifeless form on the bed. "Forgive me, Roderick, for not being here. I did love you in my own way, but life goes on and I know you wouldn't want me to drown in grief. I'm still young. It was good. You knew it, and so did I, but it's over." She straightened her shoulders and walked down to the library to face Jim Levinson, Roderick's long time friend and physician. If Jim disapproved of her absence, he didn't show it. He simply went over the details, patted her on the shoulder and left.

The funeral details had been taken care of months ago. Roderick was adamant about orchestrating his own "send off" as he referred to it. No foolish speeches by a minister who knew nothing about the life and times of Roderick Barker. No "Rock of Ages" or "Amazing Grace." Roderick had requested that one of his oldest and closest friends do an eulogy. He had requested that any of his friends and acquaintances that wished be allowed to stand and comment, or to tell a funny or amusing story about their friendship. He loved the old style jazz and blues music. At his request, Cynthia had engaged the services of a gentleman who played in a quaint little bar to handle the piano. He carried a battered old leather satchel with the contents of a lifetime of soul to bring life to those ivory keys. It was an unusual and nostalgic event with only a handful of Roderick's best friends invited to participate. Grant James had not been invited. This was Cynthia's feeble offering on the altar of fidelity.

Chapter 9

Samantha hunched over the table staring blankly into her cup of coffee as if by magic some solution would appear there. She felt as if her whole life was falling apart. Grant had shattered her comfortable world last night with the news that they were in serious financial trouble, trouble that even her healthy income could not overcome.

Samantha and Grant earned good money. Her business had really taken off this year, and Grant had been turning a nice profit for several years now. True, they had big mortgages on their houses and they drove expensive cars but so did all of their friends. How could Grant have lost all of that in such a short time? What if no one wanted to buy his Brookston stock? They could lose their home. Sadie couldn't continue at Wooster. Trey would have to attend a local college. Samantha had so hoped to send him to a private school. She knew Trey could be brilliant, but he was bored and didn't apply himself. In a private school he would not only have more stimulation; he would have more individual attention.

Grant was working later and later every night. He was taking on extra cases to try to earn more. His relationship with the children was suffering because he was never around. This was clearly causing a discipline problem with Trey. As to his relationship with Samantha, they had become like strangers. She probably wouldn't know about this "little money problem" if she hadn't asked him to buy a car for Sadie to drive to school. She remembered the scene vividly. He had begun to yell, "All you ever do is spend money, spend, spend, spend. I can't keep up with you. I'm in debt up to my ears." Samantha had been shocked and hurt by the attack. She budgeted money carefully and Grant knew that. She never made a major purchase without consulting him first. She knew something overwhelming must have happened to cause such a break in an otherwise calm man. A feeling of unease stirred in Samantha's chest. "Of course, we won't buy the car if we can't afford it, but I don't understand, Grant, I thought all our investments were doing well."

"Well, they're not," he had snarled and stalked out. Later when he returned, he seemed somewhat calmer and more collected. As a matter of fact, he seemed almost content as if a weight had been lifted. That's when he explained the magnitude of their problem, and the possible solution of selling Brookston stock.

Samantha dragged herself up from the table and turned to her bedroom to dress. She had a luncheon engagement with Sally. Sally was married to Sam Warfield, a tightfisted, dour faced, old fuddy-duddy whose only vice was to occasionally gamble on a golf game. Samantha couldn't understand why a vivacious, cute person like Sally would marry such a man, especially since he was the county coroner. Samantha shuddered at the thought of living with someone who kept company with dead bodies on a regular basis. Samantha especially dreaded going today, but she just couldn't let Sally down. Sally really looked forward to their lunch dates.

Samantha opened the door at Vestigees to find Sally inside. Sally was cute and petite. Her dark hair tumbled around her shoulders creating a frame for her luminous brown eyes and Miss America smile. Today she was wearing a Laura Ashley dress that made her look very young and innocent. She was in direct contrast to the sophisticated business image reflected by Samantha.

"Hi, Sally, sorry to be running late. I just couldn't get going today."

"Aren't you feeling well?" Sally asked solicitously.

"I'm okay," Samantha replied, "just a little tired. I was up late last night. I waited up for Grant." Samantha wondered why she impulsively added this.

"Oh," said Sally, "is he working on a case that's keeping him late?"

Samantha thought quickly, "Yes, Roderick Barker died last month, and Grant is helping his widow put all of his affairs in order."

The maitre d' approached with the routine question, "Smoking or non-smoking, ladies?"

"Non-smoking," Samantha said quickly although she knew Sally smoked. She just couldn't bear that irritation today. Her head was already playing a marching song.

The maitre d' led them to a nice booth in the front corner. Sally was talking rapidly. She was very excited about being invited to the inaugural ball in the state capitol. This was an affair Sam would be delighted to attend because everyone who was anyone in politics would be there. Sam liked to rub elbows with politicians and it had served him well. Sam didn't earn much as county coroner but he had inherited some money from his grandmother, a trust fund, Grant had told her, that paid a tidy little sum quarterly, with some sort of provision that he could invade the principal for investment purposes approved by the trustee. Brookston Bank was one of the approved investments.

Sally excused herself to go to the powder room or the "little girls' room" as she referred to it. Samantha never understood why adults referred to the ladies toilet as the "little girls' room." Samantha became aware of a murmur of conversation in the next booth. Two female voices were having an animated conversation about their bosses. One of the voices sounded familiar. Just as Samantha recognized the voice and was rising to step around and greet Grant's secretary, she froze in motion. Della said, "He's having a major affair, you know."

The other voice eagerly responded, "No, I didn't know. Who is she? Someone I know, I hope!"

"I don't think so," Della replied, "she's a client. You might have seen her, small blond woman, dresses expensively but a little on the seductive side."

"On the seductive side," the other voice gushed. "Whoa! Tell me about her…it…the affair."

Samantha's heart sank, she held her breath, praying that they were not talking about Grant. "Oh, well," Della continued, "she always comes late afternoon and, after he has me get her something to drink, he tells me I can leave and shuts the door."

"How can you be sure they're having an affair?"

Della laughed, "A secretary has a way of knowing, like American Express bills, for example."

"You don't look at his personal bills," the other voice sounded shocked.

"No," Della replied quickly, "but I pay his company credit card bills, and he has to specify the client. He takes her to dinner out of town." Della's voice underscored the significance of this behavior.

At this moment Sally returned. She took one look at Samantha and said, "Samantha, you're white as a sheet, are you okay?"

Samantha replied weakly, "I do feel ill. I think I should go home." She felt like she was smothering. If she didn't get out in the fresh air she was going to faint. She felt panic rising in her throat. She couldn't face Della now. Sally signaled the maitre d' while Samantha rushed outside.

Chapter 10

Samantha was bone tired. She had not slept well last night and tonight's monthly Business and Professional Women's meeting had been the last straw. She'd had a rough day. The meeting had been one of those irritating times when Charlotte and Donna bickered constantly. They never agreed on anything. She was really ready for this year to be over so she could pass the presidency on to someone else. Next year she planned to be less active.

Samantha dropped her purse on the couch and kicked off her shoes. Her feet hurt and she had a splitting headache. Why did there have to be days like this. All she wanted to do was jump in a hot tub and soak. Then she planned to slip on her comfortable old flannel pajamas and prop her feet up. She welcomed the solitude of the house. Sadie was away at college. Trey was working on the school float for the Christmas parade. Grant, as usual, was working late. Samantha sank into the recliner and leaned back. She needed to think. She was exhausted. She had not slept well this past week since Grant dropped the bomb about the poor state of their financial situation. She had always trusted Grant's judgment; but the last several investments they made had been unfortunate, and now she wasn't sure where Sadie's college fund stood. Why had life become so difficult?

For years Samantha had considered herself so lucky to have the perfect life, a handsome loving husband, two great children, financial stability and good social standing in the community. Lately, several things had bothered her. She had felt uneasy for some time. Intuitively, she had known something wasn't right. Her life wasn't as satisfying as it had once been. The children were growing up and didn't make as many demands on her. While that was a relief, it also left her feeling a little weird. She couldn't quite define her feelings. A frown formed on her brow as her thoughts turned to Grant. She had always trusted him, but now it appeared that had been unwise. It had never occurred to her that he might be unfaithful. She still wouldn't believe it if she hadn't heard Della with her own ears. She knew he loved her or, at least, he had. Her mind was going in circles. She realized she had been holding her breath and gasped for air. Was this possibly just a middle age fling or had he fallen out of love with her? Tears stung her eyes. How could she have been so blind? Had she driven him away unknowingly? It had been a long time since he had brought her flowers or a special card. When had he last sneaked up behind her and nibbled on her neck? Recently, their lovemaking had not been particularly passionate or romantic. What was it then? Obligation? Duty? She hated the thought of that possibility. It had always been so tender, so fierce, so exciting, and so wonderful.

Samantha felt as if she were trapped in a bad dream. Why had she not seen it? It was true. Grant was seeing another woman. The pain of it seized her on the soul level. She felt dizzy and nauseous. It all added up. The late nights at the office; the match book cover from "Rose's;" the reddish-brown smear on Grant's overcoat; and that client he was with the day she ran into him outside his office, that striking blond with whom he'd had lunch. What was the name, Barker...Cynthia Barker. Samantha remembered Cynthia's smile. There was something about that smile which bothered her. Samantha covered her eyes with her hand trying to block out the vision of Cynthia. It can't be. Not after twenty-two years of marriage. How could this be happening to her? Maybe she was overreacting. No! Della's words rang in her mind. Della never gossiped. She wouldn't have told Judge Henry's secretary if she wasn't sure. Samantha shook her head to clear it. Maybe they were talking about another attorney. Grant had never been unfaithful. He wouldn't do that. He loved his children. He would never jeopardize their love and respect.

Samantha knew she was kidding herself. She had seen them together on two occasions, in front of Grant's office and last Thursday at the Waterfall Restaurant where she was meeting a client for dinner. Grant had been quick to explain; they had been working on the distribution of Cynthia's late husband's estate and decided to take a break. In hindsight, Samantha didn't believe that for a minute. Grant had always conducted business in the office in a very professional manner. He didn't take clients to dinner. He only went to dinner with his investment buddies.

Even as Samantha tried to justify Grant's actions, her emotions overwhelmed her. She did not try to suppress the sobs. She needed the release. She would decide what to do later. Now she was giving in to her pain.

Exhausted, Samantha drifted to sleep, but was jarred awake by Grant's voice. Grant was standing over her with an expression she could not quite read. "Samantha, are you all right? Are you ill? Why aren't you in bed?"

Samantha knew she had to confront him now. She pulled herself out of the recliner. Reaching deep inside for strength and turning toward Grant she spoke softly, "We must talk."

Grant stiffened. Years of living with Samantha made him recognize the seriousness of her tone. "What's happened? Is something wrong with one of the children?"

"No," she stated, "something is wrong with us."

Samantha was not one to beat around the bush. Grant dropped his eyes hoping to hide his guilt. He knew that Samantha suspected. How could he lie to her? They had never kept secrets. He didn't know how it had happened. He had never been unfaithful before. He didn't want to hurt her. He still loved her in his own way, but things had gone too far now. Cynthia excited him, made him feel alive.

Realizing he had paused too long, Grant replied, "What do you mean?" Grant knew full well what she meant but was stalling for time.

"Grant, don't deny it. It all adds up. You're having an affair with Cynthia Barker. I need to know why. How could you destroy all we have together? Why?" Samantha's voice cracked as she felt her control slipping. It hurt to think of Grant with another woman.

Grant was shaken. They had a good life. Samantha had been a good wife and an outstanding mother. He had always put his family first. He hadn't expected to feel so confused. He would always love Samantha, but he needed Cynthia. He had to think about himself for a change. Cynthia understood. His needs were important to her. With barely a whisper Grant replied, "I don't know. It just happened. I didn't plan it."

"Promise me it won't happen again. We'll go to counseling. Promise me, Grant!" Samantha waited breathlessly needing Grant to reassure her, tell her she was mistaken and he still loved her. Grant remained silent, so torn with emotion he couldn't speak. What had he done? How could he walk out on his family? What would his parents think? What a mess he had made. He needed to talk to Cynthia. She would make him feel better. She would understand. He needed to get out of here.

"Samantha, this isn't all my fault. If things were right with us, it wouldn't have happened. You don't know I'm around most of the time," he retorted as he tried to justify his actions.

Samantha couldn't believe her ears. "How dare you blame me," she replied hotly. "*You aren't around* most of the time." She spoke softly now.

"That's it." Grant shouted grabbing his coat and storming out the door. Samantha leaned against the door trembling and watched him drive away feeling as if he had ripped her heart out.

The hours dragged by but Grant didn't return. With each tick of the clock Samantha felt her panic rise. How could this be happening? She didn't even consider going to bed. She knew sleep was impossible. Her whole world was crashing in on her.

In all these years the thought of Grant's being unfaithful had never entered her mind. The taste of betrayal was so bitter it was choking her. "Where is he? Is he with Cynthia? How could he do this after all we have meant to each other? Where did I fail?" Samantha's mind was tormented with doubts and unanswered questions. Her heart was an open wound. The pain was so intense that it would surely kill her. "Should I try to find him? Why doesn't he call to say he is sorry?" She picked up the phone to assure herself it wasn't out of order. A sob escaped and she crumpled into the corner. She was falling apart and she had to accept the fact that Grant was not coming back tonight. Would he be back at all?

As he drove off Grant had no clear plan in mind. He would like to talk with Cynthia but his guilt wouldn't let him call. He needed to think. How had he gotten himself in such a mess? He had always been so together. How could he love two women? He still did love Samantha but he loved Cynthia differently. Too much of a good thing. It reminded him of the first time he had indulged in alcohol. It had been a hot summer day at the lake with a couple of buddies. They were all underage but had persuaded Jake's big brother to buy them a case of beer. Man, that ice-cold beer was great. He couldn't wait to have another, then another. He remembered feeling like a real stud until his stomach decided to reject it. Jeez, he thought he was going to die. In fact, he had hoped he would for a while. That's how he felt now. He had hurt and disappointed his mom and dad then and now he was hurting Samantha. She had trusted him just as his parents had that time long ago. How could he feel repulsed by his action and lust for Cynthia all at the same time? "She makes me feel young again," he rationalized.

Grant realized he had been on autopilot and was now parked in front of his office. He could stay here tonight and sleep on the couch. He always kept toiletries, shaving gear, clean underwear, and a shirt here for those times he was tied up with last minute preparations for a tough case. Grant had experienced a lot of disappointments lately. His investment disaster had left his ego severely bruised. That case he lost last week still galled him. He had gotten careless and underestimated his opponent. He had too much on his mind. It had destroyed his concentration. He had to make a choice. He knew he couldn't have it both ways. Samantha had been a good wife and mother. It wasn't her fault the excitement was gone. They lived very demanding lives. They had drifted apart. On the other hand, Cynthia made him feel like a new man. He looked forward to their time together. She was fun, sexy, daring and so good in the sack. She had him performing like a young stud again. She made him feel like he could walk on water, and he really needed that kind of adulation right now. Samantha had thought he was invincible but that was years ago. "A man has to grab the brass ring when it is offered, and Cynthia is holding it out to me," he rationalized again.

Grant became aware he had been chain smoking. The ashtray was overflowing. The whole office reeked of it. Della would have a fit when she came in. Grant had begun smoking again after he met Cynthia. Samantha was strongly opposed to smoking so he had refrained from letting her know that he had taken up the habit again. He knew it was only a matter of time before she noticed it on his breath. She had already commented about how his clients' smoke was clinging to his clothing. Grant looked at the clock. "Three-thirty," he exclaimed aloud, "I've got to get some sleep." He had to be in court at nine a.m. and still needed to review the details of his case. Grant stripped down to his briefs and stretched out on the couch. The last thing he remembered was hearing the four a.m. Burlington Express whistle through town.

Chapter 11

Samantha had a sleepless night. She had forgotten how it felt to wake up feeling good. She was like a robot. Pouring herself a cup of coffee, she leaned against the cabinet. She was still wearing her gown. She just didn't have the energy or the will to get dressed. Her eyes were drawn to the papers on the table. Her lawyer had sent them over this morning. She stared at the papers with glazed eyes, still as death. That's how she felt...dead. Grant's words echoed in her ears with a deafening roar. She pressed her hands across her ears trying to silence them, but the words kept reverberating. "I want a divorce...I want a divorce...I want a divorce." She still couldn't believe it. How had this happened? It was a bad dream. She'd wake up soon and Grant would reassure her, profess his undying love, take her in his arms and make, mad, passionate love to her. Grant was an excellent lover. She felt her body respond as she remembered his touch. Grant took his time. He was a slow, patient lover pushing her over the edge until she screamed for release. Together they soared, then plunged into blissful warmth.

Whirling around she poured a cup of coffee. "Damn! Damn him to hell. How could he leave me for that bitch." Samantha shuddered at the thought. Grant had said cruel and hurtful things. How could she still love him? She had never known he was capable of such meanness. That woman had twisted his mind. She was evil and manipulative...a witch. No, bitch was a better word for her. How low can you get to have an affair while your ailing husband lies dying? How could Grant love a woman like that? They deserved each other.

Samantha remembered her first meeting with Cynthia. She had been to the bookstore near Grant's office and had decided to drop in. As she had approached his building, she spotted him walking toward her. He had an attractive woman with him. She was a petite blond with an eye-catching figure. Samantha had felt a sudden jolt of jealousy. She had scolded herself for stupid thoughts. Grant smiled and waved. They waited for her to join them. Grant introduced the woman as his client, Cynthia Barker. She and her husband were having a last will and testament prepared. Samantha mentally noted the woman's mode of dress. Expensive, no doubt a designer label, but a little too revealing for her taste. An electric blue, lycra suit cut very low exposing considerable cleavage. The skintight skirt was only inches longer than the jacket. Samantha felt sure that, if the woman bent over, little would be left to the imagination. Samantha wondered briefly if she wore anything underneath. Looking back Samantha realized everything about the woman shouted seductress. Samantha remembered noticing that Cynthia had been studying her intently. There had been something unsettling about the woman. Samantha excused herself not wanting to intrude when Grant was with a client.

Samantha hadn't thought too much of the incident. It seemed innocent enough. However, she recalled the second meeting with a heavy heart. It replayed in her mind like a movie. She had agreed to meet a new client at the Waterfall Restaurant for dinner. The couple had just moved from Minneapolis and bought an older home. They wanted to renovate it with Samantha's help. The seller, a member of BPWA, referred the couple to her. She normally didn't tie up her evenings with clients, but she had made an exception to accommodate them. As she pulled into the parking lot she thought she saw Grant's car. She dismissed it as a similar vehicle. She knew he never ate dinner when he worked late.

As the maitre d' showed Samantha to her table, she was surprised to see Grant and Cynthia. They were in deep conversation. They seemed very comfortable. On second thought, there was an air of intimacy. Samantha felt a sudden chill as she moved in slow motion. Not liking what she was seeing, she denied the anxiety rising in her. What was Grant doing here alone with that woman? Grant, sensing a presence, looked up. He sprang to his feet momentarily stunned. Was that guilt that flashed across his face? Quickly recovering, he said, "Samantha, what are you doing here? You remember Mrs. Barker. We were just taking a break. We're working on the distribution of her late husband's estate."

The sudden rush of suspicion and resentment surprised Samantha. She had never been jealous of Grant. He had never given her any reason. She quickly composed herself, but not before she saw the flicker of amusement cross Cynthia's face. "I'm meeting a couple to discuss renovating the older home they have just purchased. In fact, I see them now. I'll see you later at the house. Nice seeing you, Mrs. Barker. I'm sorry to hear of your loss."

Samantha remembered that Grant and Cynthia had quickly finished their meal and left. Afterward, she had found it difficult to concentrate on her new clients.

Suddenly, Samantha realized she had been staring into space for some time. Her coffee was cold and her fingers ached from clutching the cup so tightly.

Sighing, she sat down to review the divorce settlement. Divorce was not what she wanted. She wanted her husband and children together. Samantha had strong feelings about divorce. She had been reared a Catholic and her religion held that marriage was "until death do us part." She didn't want to give up so easily, but Grant had made it clear that he only wanted a new life with Cynthia. She could not force him to give their marriage another chance. He had flatly refused to consider counseling. Unfortunately, there had been bitter feelings and cruel words. She had tried to protect Sadie and Trey as much as possible. They were hurt and confused. Neither understood why it had happened. She had to fight an urge to shout that their dad was a jerk. She had no one. She had to be careful with Grandmother and Grandfather James. They were upset and angry with Grant for breaking up his family, but after all he was their son. They had always liked her, but she didn't want to burden them further.

Reluctantly, she read the decree and found it in order. She would receive alimony for two years. She could keep the house in town and she had her children. Grant would provide partial support for Trey and help with Sadie's college. For that she was grateful. With a feeling of finality, she signed away life as she had known it.

Chapter 12

Cynthia heard the phone ringing as she flew down the stairs, "Mildred, Mildred, where are you? Do I have to do everything myself?" She grabbed the phone. "Hello."

"This is she."

"Ten o'clock will be fine." Cynthia slammed the phone back onto its cradle. "Where is that girl?" Cynthia felt irritated. What was the point of having servants if they were never around? The photographer would be here soon, and she needed help with her dress.

Cynthia stopped in front of the big hall mirror and looked critically at herself. She looked a little stressed. Roderick had been dead for just over a year now. All that sitting by his bed holding his hand had taken a toll on her. She had aged. She looked at the tiny downward lines at the corners of her mouth. When this wedding was over, she would take a month in Greenbrook Spa and see Dr. Charles for a little nip and tuck. Cynthia thought fondly of the plastic surgeon. She had considered him as a possible partner before Roderick, but decided he knew too much about her.

The doorbell rang. It was Patti, Cynthia's wedding coordinator, who regularly spent time carrying out Cynthia's directions. Patti realized very early that Cynthia would call all the shots on this wedding. Patti would be at most an errand girl and at worst someone to blame for any and all problems that might arise. There was really no need for her to be here today. The photographer was coming to make a portrait of the bride in her gown. It seemed to Patti a bit tacky to be having a third marriage in a long white gown. Cynthia had told her that she was just recently widowed for the second time. Patti felt that Cynthia had certainly wasted no time in finding a replacement for her late husband. She did not like Cynthia and normally would not have taken this wedding, but she needed the money. Her son wanted to study for a year in Paris. He was a very talented artist and could benefit from a year at the Ecole d' Beaux Arts.

"Where are we going to shoot this photograph?" Cynthia's demanding voice broke Patti's reverie. Patti knew full well that Cynthia had planned to use the staircase.

"I think the staircase would be a lovely setting." Patti swept her eyes over the huge foyer, which was dominated by a massive winding staircase. The rails were highly polished cherry wood. The cherry wood treads were covered down the center with a deep burgundy carpet. The floor was of travertine marble. Cynthia was obviously pleased that Patti had chosen the same as she. What she didn't know was that Patti's experience told her to check the placement of the flowers in order to know where the bride wanted to be photographed. In the

Barker foyer this morning, flowers were heavily situated on either side of the staircase newel posts.

"Perhaps, you should slip into your dress," Patti suggested.

"I'll need you to help me," Cynthia stated imperiously. "I can't find that worthless Mildred."

Patti sighed softly and followed Cynthia up the stairs. Patti's eyes didn't miss much as she entered the large bedroom. The room was elegantly furnished with expensive, solid woods, hand carved and highly polished. On the bed was a duvet cover of fine silk in a soft beige with an embroidered pattern in a slightly deeper color. The bridal gown was hanging on a special rack in the center of the room. The entire rack was padded with white silk and beaded with tiny pearls. She must have had it made especially for this occasion. "Talk about overkill!" Patti thought.

The dress was stunning. It was pure white silk satin cut straight across the top front and back and held together at the shoulders with tiny spaghetti straps. The bodice was fitted to the hips at which point it gracefully flowed into an A-line. The back was closed with tiny covered buttons to the base of the hips at which point the skirt split revealing a four-foot tulle train. The dress was clearly a designer dress, probably a Vera Wang.

Cynthia had slipped out of her slacks and appeared ready to begin donning the bridal gown. Patti reached for the gown. "No, no, not yet," Cynthia stopped her, "I have to take a shower."

Patti wondered how she was going to protect that long mop of hair while she showered. "I'll just wait downstairs," she offered.

"No, stay here, I might need you." Cynthia ordered.

Patti felt resentment. A retort rose to her lips but she swallowed it. Her contract did not include being Cynthia's personal maid. Cynthia had not waited for her reply. Water was already running in the shower.

Patti walked around the room looking at the paintings, photographs, and other objects occupying space in this room. There was no evidence that Cynthia's dead husband ever had lived in this room, for that matter, in this house as far as Patti had seen. She noticed the open drawer at the bedside. Curiosity propelled her to the nightstand. She stood staring at the contents. She was amazed at the jumbled drawer. "Cynthia is so meticulous about everything," Patti thought, "I'm surprised her nightstand drawer is such a mess. Maybe that is what she's like…neat as a pin on the outside but a disaster inside." Patti picked up a medicine bottle that she noticed had Cynthia's dead husband's name on it. "Digitoxin, I wonder what that's for," Patti mused, "probably a pain killer or sleeping tablet. Otherwise, she would have disposed of it when she cleared out the rest of his belongings." She placed the bottle back in the drawer and moved away feeling a little like a peeping tom.

Cynthia emerged from the bathroom toweling herself dry. Her makeup and hair looked as if they hadn't been touched. How in the world had she managed that in a shower? Patti started to remark on what she considered nothing short of a miracle, but she thought better of it. She really didn't want to know this woman better, and she certainly didn't want to pay her a compliment.

Patti started as the doorbell rang. "I'll get that," she breathed a sigh of relief as she hurried from the room. Mildred stood at the bottom of the staircase. With her was a thin young man. He was good looking in a pale sort of way, hair thinning on the top and long limp ponytail behind.

"Hi, I'm Patti Burleson, the coordinator. You are Charlie." It was a statement not a question.

Charlie smiled, "Where should I set up my equipment?"

It was clear that he knew the choice of setting was not his. Patti wondered if he needed money, too. Of course, he did. She knew the type. Artistic, very proud of his work, perfectionistic, took too many shots in order to get a perfect one, and then didn't charge enough for prints because he wanted as many people as possible to have a sample of his work.

Patti sent Mildred to help Cynthia. A half-hour later Cynthia appeared at the head of the stairs and stood in a manner, which could only be described as "striking a pose." She held the position until she felt sure her stunning beauty had been fully appreciated.

"Mildred, please lift my train and veil carefully," she ordered, "I do not want them wrinkled." On that note she moved regally down the stairs. The young photographer was obviously awestruck.

"It's possible that in his young life he has never seen such beauty," Patti admitted grudgingly. Mildred looked panicked. She was clearly trying to see how she could pass Cynthia without rumpling the gown. Patti stepped forward and relieved her of the veil and train. A grateful Mildred retreated up the stairs. Patti nudged the mesmerized photographer into action.

~ ~ ~ ~ ~ ~ ~ ~ ~ ~ ~ ~ ~ ~ ~ ~

Sunday dawned bright and warm. Cynthia had been up since six. She was exhilarated. This was it. She had waited a long time for this. She had always wanted a big wedding. Her previous two husbands had insisted they have a small quiet ceremony, but Grant had been more understanding. At first he had resisted but she had won him over. She had envisioned the day in her mind. First, she was to have a massage and a facial. Next, she was scheduled for a manicure and a pedicure. Her hair appointment followed and finally her makeup session. "While I'm having my pedicure, I'll eat a light snack. I want my stomach very flat for this wedding." Cynthia was very pleased with her trim body.

Cynthia had instructed Grant not to come around or call. She didn't want him to see her before the wedding. That would be bad luck. Cynthia planned to wear a blue garter. She had laid out the set of pearls that had belonged to her grandmother. She thought fondly of her grandmother. Mama Hamilton had been gone for many years now, but Cynthia had been very close to her and still missed her. It was a shame she had a sudden heart attack while she was still young, only 65. Cynthia had received a small inheritance from her. That money had helped to build the image that Cynthia had used to mesmerize Buck, her first husband.

Cynthia had checked the flowers in the church last night. Kirby had done a wonderful job. She had decided on all white flowers, roses, lilies and sprays of dendrobian orchids. This was going to be the most magnificent wedding. Cynthia looked at her watch and refilled her cup. She did love a good cup of herbal tea.

~ ~ ~ ~ ~ ~ ~ ~ ~ ~ ~ ~ ~ ~ ~ ~

Cynthia watched the guests arriving. She had invited all Grant and Roderick's business associates and their families. She felt a certain amount of smug satisfaction in knowing that all of Grant and Roderick's associates would show up. They wouldn't want to jeopardize the business relationship regardless of what they felt personally. The church would be full. "Damn," Cynthia thought, "I love being wealthy." People seldom turned you down when you invited them socially or asked them a favor. It made Cynthia feel very powerful.

Chapter 13

Cynthia sat across the desk from Brent Spencer. His success as an insurance broker was apparent by his elaborate surroundings. The intricately carved golden oak partners' desk and matching credenza were a priceless treasure. Soft honey gold leather side chairs blended beautifully with the warm, earthy atmosphere. The rich oak paneled walls cast a warm glow throughout the room.

The walls were adorned with original works in gilded frames depicting the mid-1800s. The entire room was decorated for the simple purpose of creating a feeling of comfort, trust, and protection. It was no wonder Brent was so very successful. He had all your senses responding while he worked his professional magic. The thick, dark piney green carpet with the shimmer of velvet had an allure that almost whispered, "Touch me, let me caress your soft skin." For a moment Cynthia envisioned her creamy, white skin against the velvety dark and piney woods, and felt the soft fibers brush her nipples. Deep within she felt a stir of arousal. She secretly wondered if Brent had ever given in to the tantalizing seduction of it.

She had first met Brent when she and Roderick had purchased their policies shortly after their marriage. Roderick had been a very wealthy man, but an additional one million had been further security for Cynthia's future. It was a very different story with Grant, considering his crippled financial condition. He had explained to her how one of his investments had gone sour leaving him with limited assets. Then his divorce from Samantha had depleted them further. Cynthia wasn't worried, she was sure he would regain his losses rapidly. He was considered one of the leading attorneys in town. He had the earning power to become financially comfortable. Besides she had contacts that would be beneficial to him. However, she never took chances. Last night she had suggested that they each purchase life insurance policies for one million dollars. He had agreed, but was hesitant about making her the sole beneficiary. She quickly had pointed out that he was her sole beneficiary. He was concerned about his children. She assured him she would always look after his children in the event something happened to him. "I will use part of the money for trust funds," she reassured him. They would not want for anything. After much discussion he had finally decided to sell the country house and invest in stock portfolios for both children therefore securing a legacy for them. She had approached the subject of their wills and he agreed to draft a copy for her approval. After all, they were young, so there was not any big hurry he had teased her. He then began a slow game of seduction, guiding her gently toward the giant sized marble Jacuzzi.

Grinning wickedly he said, "Let me show you what a young man can do for you."

"You're on, big boy. I might just love you to death." Cynthia purred seductively.

Chapter 14

Samantha wandered through the house. The silence was deafening. She could remember the time when she welcomed the solitude, now she found it oppressive. She noticed that her plants were drooping. She hadn't given them her usual careful attention lately. Feeling a little guilty she filled a pitcher with water and set about remedying the signs of her neglect.

Sadie had gone back to college in Ohio. Samantha really missed her. They were very close, mother, daughter, and best friends. Sadie had always been very mature. Samantha could discuss anything with her. Only she knew how much Samantha still missed Grant. Samantha had no one to talk to now. Trey was too young to understand her feelings. He was having his own problems coping with the absence of his father. Samantha thanked God she still had Trey at home. She didn't have to face being totally alone. She wasn't sure what she would do when the time came. She didn't even want to think about it. Shivering, she prayed it was true that time heals a broken heart. Samantha suppressed a sob. It still hurt so much. She felt so betrayed. "Oh God, what has happened to my perfect life? What have I done to deserve this?" For the first time in her life, Samantha's faith in God was tested. She couldn't stop herself from questioning why He had deserted her family. Hadn't they lived a good moral life, helped their neighbors and the less fortunate. They didn't abuse their bodies, didn't hate anyone, and tried to treat everyone equally. They respected God and His universe. Why was her family suffering so?

Samantha especially worried about Trey. He had changed. He was so moody. She rarely saw him smile anymore. He had always been so carefree and happy. She hoped his grades were not slipping further. He wasn't a star student at best. He couldn't risk letting down or he would jeopardize his sports position. She knew he missed his father terribly. Even though Grant had worked long hours, he always spent time with Trey on weekends. She could almost hear them out back shooting basketball goals.

The doorbell startled Samantha. "Who could that be?" Trey was at gymnastics. Puzzled, she peeked through the window. She stiffened when she realized Grant's car was in the driveway. What was he doing here? What could he possibly want? Steeling herself, Samantha opened the door. Unable to speak, she just stared at Grant. How strange it felt to have him here. Grant shuffled from one foot to the other.

"May I come in?" he asked softly.

Still clutching the door, Samantha nodded and stepped aside. Grant stepped into the entry hall and faced her waiting for her to speak. He felt very uncomfortable, but he had promised Trey. Grant ran his fingers through his hair the way he always did when he was nervous. Samantha recognized his discomfort. "Let him squirm," she thought. She squared her shoulders and stared at him.

Clearing his throat, Grant said, "We need to talk about Trey."

"What about Trey?" Samantha asked.

"He called me this afternoon," Grant said staring at his shoes.

"What did he want? Is something wrong?" Samantha couldn't keep the anxiety out of her voice.

Grant paused, dreading her reaction. "He asked if he could live with me," he answered cautiously.

Samantha was visibly shaken. Surely, she had not heard him correctly. "Did you say Trey asked to live with you?" It was no more than a whisper.

"Yes," Grant replied.

Bewildered, Samantha shook her head. "But, he hasn't said a word to me."

"He didn't want to hurt you. He has evidently been thinking about it for some time. He said he had talked with his school counselor."

Grant continued to stare at his feet. He couldn't even look her in the eye. He knew the hurt he would see there. He cared for her and hated to hurt her further. He still felt guilty about leaving. How could you care as much as he did and still leave? He didn't understand it, but he couldn't change it now.

Samantha fought the suffocating feeling in her throat. Grant wouldn't lie about one of the children. Her knuckles whitened as she increased her grip on the door. "He can't do that," she choked. "I won't let him." Her control was slipping. She didn't want to break down in front of Grant. She needed to think. Grant sensed her panic.

Meeting her eyes, he said, "He's almost nineteen. He's old enough to know where he wants to live. Don't make this any more difficult than it already is, Samantha. Please don't fight it."

Samantha's mind raced. Why hadn't Trey talked with her? Had he stopped loving her, too? Oh God, how much more could she take? She'd have no one. Everyone she loved was gone. "Dear God, give me strength," she silently prayed. Realizing Grant was staring at her, Samantha's head snapped up. "I need time to think about this. I want to talk with Trey before I make my decision. I'll call your office tomorrow."

Grant took a hesitant step toward her with a strange expression on his face. In that split second Samantha thought, hoped, that he was going to take her in his arms. She had to get him out of there before she fell apart. She moved toward the door. Grant turned slowly and followed her. He thought how nice it would be to pull her into his arms and hold her, how familiar and comfortable. He knew how distressed she was, but he didn't have the right to do that now.

"That will be fine, call me in the afternoon. I'm in court all morning," he said softly and closed the door behind him.

Samantha made it to the couch before collapsing in gut wrenching sobs. How could she give up her beloved son? She didn't want to make this more difficult for him. She knew he was hurting, too. She knew her son loved her very much. It must have been terrible for him to make this decision. She wouldn't force him to stay. Grant was right, she knew that he was old enough to choose. She just hadn't been prepared for this. Thinking back, she realized she had been ignoring the signs. Trey missed his father, and he was at the age when adolescent hormones were raging. It was easier to discuss those problems with a father. Trey had complained that it was difficult to have time alone with his dad on weekends, because Cynthia was always there. She understood his need, but how was she going to survive without him? She had lost so much already.

Much later, she climbed the stairs and went to Trey's room. Slowly, she circled the room picking up his prized possessions, his school trophies, reliving each memory.

Samantha did not know how long she had been clutching Trey's picture. Sensing his presence, she turned to see Trey standing in the doorway. He had been unable to speak because of the lump in his throat. He found it hard to breathe. Trey loved his mother so much, but he needed his dad right now. There were things that only a dad could tell him. It tied him in knots to think he was hurting her. She was a wonderful mother, and she was always there for him. He felt like he was betraying her just as his dad had done, but he missed his dad so much. Samantha smiled through her tears.

"I'll miss you, Trey. I love you very much. It's going to be lonesome without you."

Trey crossed the room in three steps and threw his arms around her. "I'm so sorry, Mom. You know how much I love you, but I miss Dad. I really need him right now. I'll just be across town. I'll come over anytime you need me. I promise, I'll call everyday."

They stood in silent embrace until Samantha drew back brushing his hair off his forehead. "I'll help you pack in the morning. You'll need to decide what you want to take to your dad's. Goodnight, sweetheart, I love you."

"Goodnight, Mom, I love you, too, and thanks for understanding."

~ ~ ~ ~ ~ ~ ~ ~ ~ ~ ~ ~ ~ ~ ~ ~

Early the next morning the phone rang. "Good morning, Samantha. I hope I didn't awaken you." It was Grandmother James. Why was she calling so early? She was never up before at least ten a.m. Suddenly, it hit Samantha. Margaret knew about Trey's moving in with his dad and Cynthia. Samantha's jaw tightened. "Good morning, Margaret. What are you doing up so early?"

"Samantha, I had the urge to have lunch at the Terrace Room. I love their chicken salad and I've been obsessing about their baked fudge. How about it, can you get away?"

Samantha had a million things to do, but she realized Margaret was reaching out. She wanted Samantha to know she understood the emotional turmoil concerning Trey.

"Sure, Margaret, do you want me to pick you up or shall we meet there?" Margaret said she had several errands, so she would meet Samantha at eleven forty-five a.m. at the restaurant.

Samantha rummaged through her closet trying to decide what to wear. She had lost weight and most of her clothes were beginning to hang on her. She really needed to go shopping. Maybe after lunch she would do that. She could use a boost, and a new outfit or two always did the trick, at least temporarily.

When Samantha arrived Margaret had already taken a table. Waving for Samantha to join her, Margaret watched her approach with approval. She admired Samantha very much. She always looked so fresh and classy. She was dressed in tan silk slacks, raw silk tweed jacket, pale cream silk shirt and a soft brown leather loafer. Samantha wore very little jewelry; small gold hoops adorned her ears. Her makeup was almost invisible giving her a fresh natural appearance. She looked much younger than her 42 years. Margaret loved the warmth she felt from those hazel eyes. There was always a twinkle hiding in them. Her dark ash brown hair enhanced that fresh natural look. Margaret had been very pleased with her son's choice. After the usual greetings, they placed their orders.

Margaret immediately reached for Samantha's hand, "I talked with Grant last night, dear. He told me about Trey. I want you to know, I think you are a wonderful mother. Trey loves you; he just needs his dad right now. He'll always be close to you and will always be there for you. So will I, Samantha! Don't ever forget that. You were my son's first choice and Dad and I agreed one hundred percent. We haven't changed our minds; but Grant has married Cynthia, and we can't change that either. You understand, don't you?"

Samantha swallowed hard, choking on her emotion. "I know, Margaret, and I respect your feelings. I know Trey loves me and I would never force him to stay with me, if he would rather…if he needs to be with his father. I'll just have to find a way to cope." Fighting to maintain control, Samantha added, "I've been thinking about taking a sculpting course at the college, maybe now is the time to do that."

Margaret squeezed her hand and gave her a grateful smile as their food arrived. They ate their meal in a more or less uneasy silence broken by occasional bits of small talk.

"Bradford's is having a great sale. You should stop by there this afternoon," commented Samantha.

"I can't. Forest is packing for another of his bass tournaments."

"Well, tell him I said to catch enough for all of us. You know how much I love fresh fish." They felt much more than they were saying, but both knew circumstances inhibited their free exchange of emotions. The baked fudge arrived breaking the tension. They savored the decadence of the dessert.

Peter Stanton was seated across the room and had observed Samantha's arrival. He had found her very attractive from the moment they met. He remembered how awestruck he was when she arrived at his house last year, windblown, beautiful, and loaded down with sample books. She radiated energy and brought sunshine into the room even though the weather had suddenly turned wintry. She was delightful, easy to talk to, and had a wonderful laugh. Before she left that day, they had formed an unspoken bond. They discovered many common interests and were talking like old friends. He had not felt that comfortable with a woman in years. His only regret was that she was married, and instinctively he knew she was not the type to have a clandestine affair. To be honest, he didn't want that either. If he ever had a woman like her in his life, he wanted it on very different terms.

Watching, he wondered who the older woman was. They seemed to be engaged in intense, no, very emotional conversation. He could read it in their expressions. Samantha was trying hard to appear calm, but she didn't hide her feelings well. "What has upset this beautiful lady?" he wondered. He would go over and say hello before he left. He didn't want to intrude now. He sensed their conversation was too private to invade. He hoped Samantha wasn't ill. She didn't look pale or sick. However, she did appear thinner than he remembered, and he remembered everything about her. She was frequently in his thoughts. Maybe, it was his forty-fifth coming up that was getting to him. He had not seriously considered a permanent relationship since Amy's death in Scotland eleven years ago. He was thankful that nightmare was finally fading. They had married so young and grown up together. When her dream vacation with her old college roommates had turned out to be her last, he was devastated. How he had missed her. Pulling his thoughts back to the present, he saw the waiter bring dessert to Samantha and her friend. Deciding to approach her now, he started down the stairs just as she raised her head. Their eyes met and she gave him a brilliant smile. His heart skipped a beat. This woman definitely had a profound effect on him.

Samantha smiled as he approached. She hadn't seen Peter Stanton since she decorated his home sometime last year. She had thought of him far too often after that. He was handsome as ever. Was that a little gray showing at his temples? It was obvious he had not neglected his outdoor activities. He was as bronze as a Greek god. "Wait until he turns that devilish smile on Margaret. She will melt! That's what he does to me," she realized with a start. This man could be dangerous. She hoped Margaret didn't notice how he affected her. She wasn't sure how Margaret would react to her being attracted to another man.

Blinding her with one of his smiles, he grasp her hand. "Samantha, it is so good to see you. I should have known you would like the Terrace Room. It's one of my favorite places."

"It's good to see you, too, Peter. It's been awhile." Basking in his gaze, she remembered Margaret. "I'd like you to meet my mother, ah, my ex-mother-in-law, Margaret James. Margaret, this is Peter Stanton. I decorated his home this past year." As they exchanged pleasantries, Samantha could tell Margaret was impressed. She was right, Peter was an instant charmer. As Peter left, Margaret raised her eyebrows, and commented on what an attractive man he was and asked if he was married. Samantha explained she had met him last year. According to her client, who had referred Peter, he was not married and had not been in a serious relationship since his move to Centerview ten years ago.

As Peter left the restaurant, there was a spring in his step, and a slight smile touched his face. He felt lighthearted. He hadn't missed the "ex-mother-in-law" introduction. He wondered when that happened and how he had missed it. Of course, he had been traveling a lot this year. He would make some discreet inquiries to verify when her marital status had changed before he called her. He fully intended to call her. If she were available, he didn't want someone else moving in on her. "She is a special lady," he thought. "Hungry wolves will be stalking her doors." Chuckling to himself, "I'm going to be the leader of the pack."

Chapter 15

Margaret sat at the kitchen table and stared at the chair her son occupied when he was in the house. "Forest, do you think Grant is happy?"

Forest looked up from the sports page reluctantly. He hoped Margaret was not going to lapse into another one of her long diatribes on their son's marriage. She was constantly worrying about imagined situations. "Hell, why wouldn't Grant be happy?" Forest thought, "If I had that cute little piece of ass I wouldn't complain." He couldn't voice this to his wife, of course. "I don't know, Margaret, why do you ask?"

Margaret looked at him a long time before she answered. "Just an intuition I have. I've never really understood what happened between Samantha and him. He seemed happy and then they were divorced. I think it was the money problem."

Forest was instantly alert. "What money problem?"

Margaret's hand flew to her mouth, "Oh...oh...I didn't mean to...nothing you should be concerned with, dear."

"What money problem?" Forest insisted.

Margaret reluctantly told Forest of Grant's investment failures of the previous year.

"Is he still in financial trouble?" Forest was concerned and more than a little irritated. He had warned Grant about investing on insider tips. You could never win in those situations. In the first place it was illegal, and in the second place nine out of ten of those tips were inaccurate.

"No," Margaret quickly reassured him. "He sold some of his Brookston stock to Sam Warfield."

"How much did he sell?"

"I don't know exactly. Several thousand shares." Margaret felt uneasy discussing Grant's business affairs with Forest especially when they put Grant in a bad light. She decided to swing the conversation back to her original concern. "I just think that Grant is not happy. Samantha was such a nice girl."

Forest grunted his agreement. He continued perusing the sports page.

"Cynthia treats me like a servant." Margaret blurted out.

Forest was amused. "In what way does she treat you like a servant?"

"Well, for example, when I visit them, she doesn't ask me if I would like a cup of tea, she tells me she would like one, and then asks me to make it."

Forest was more amused now. "Cheeky little tart," he thought. He couldn't imagine anyone ordering Margaret around. She was very much a take-charge woman. "Why don't you tell her no," he asked smiling.

"I couldn't do that. Grant might think I don't like her."

"Well, you don't, do you?"

"It isn't that, Forest, I just don't think Grant is happy. I think he would rather be with Samantha and the children."

"Seems to me he would have stayed with them if that's where he wanted to be." Forest was tiring of the conversation.

"I overheard them arguing a few days ago," Margaret paused, "Grant said that maybe he had chosen the wrong woman."

Forest mumbled as he turned the page of his paper, "Nothing to be done about it now."

Margaret looked troubled. "I suppose you're right."

Chapter 16

Grant stood in front of the mirror grimacing, "This damn bow tie is a nuisance." Cynthia's black tie affairs were wearing thin. He was sick of them. He had always enjoyed socializing, but not every night. He was neglecting his work. He had built his practice by hard work. He was successful, but he couldn't let up now. There were far too many hungry young attorneys out there just waiting to replace you or leave you in their dust. He sure didn't want that to happen. He should be burning the midnight oil right now to research and prepare for several cases he had pending. He had explained that to Cynthia and begged her to not accept any further invitations without his approval. Damn her, he knew she hadn't forgotten, she was just spoiled and used to having her way. Back when the heat of his pants was affecting the wit of his brain, he had thought she was very caring, but the reality of it was that she was very manipulative. Why hadn't he recognized that trait? He hated manipulative people. He missed the straightforward honesty of Samantha. In fact, he longed for a quiet evening like he and Samantha had shared, discussing their day, the good and the bad. He couldn't do that with Cynthia. She made it clear by her actions that she wanted no part of problem solving. She seemed to think the only thing he needed when things weren't going right was a roll in the hay. He couldn't complain about those romps, but he needed a partner to use as a sounding board. He needed normal, everyday, intelligent feedback sometimes, not just hot sex.

He didn't know what Cynthia did with her time, besides one luncheon after another. She wasn't involved with anything of substance. She was intelligent, but didn't seem to want to utilize it. She lacked the depth he had always admired in Samantha.

Grant especially resented tonight, because he had a big case tomorrow. He needed a clear head to present the evidence. He was up against Irene Thomas and she was one hell of a lawyer. She was young, but she knew her stuff. He'd have to be on his toes or she would make a fool of him. Thank God, it wasn't Judge Henry's docket or he'd have no edge at all. Damn Cynthia for accepting this invitation. The selfish little bitch was only interested in herself. She sure didn't want to be taken off anyone's guest list. How could he have been so blind? He had always prided himself on the practice he'd built, but she didn't give a damn about making money, all she wanted to do was spend it. But then on the other hand, Roderick had left her fixed for life, while Grant still had a family that required his financial support. However, she was going through her inheritance pretty rapidly. She had purchased and lost money on the trade-in on three eighty thousand-dollar cars since they were married. When he had tried to slow her down, she reminded him that it was her money. She came home with new clothes everyday. Her closet was crammed with dresses that still had the tags attached. She loved to try them on and parade in front of him posing like a fashion model. In the beginning it was a real turn on, but now he didn't have time for that, he had a business to run. If he brought his work home, the distraction ruined his train of thought. Things were not exactly as he had envisioned them. "As they say," he thought, "the honeymoon is definitely over."

It hit him like a fist in the gut. He didn't like his new life. In fact, he was liking Cynthia less and less. Yes, he liked her body. She was a hot number in bed and really turned heads when she entered a room, but she lacked compassion and understanding. She didn't hold a candle to Samantha. Bile rose in his throat. He'd made a terrible mistake. He had tossed away a wonderful life, a loving wife, and his children for a piece of ass; discarded them like they were nothing, letting the "old boy" between his legs lead the way. What a fool he had been. He wondered grimly if they could ever forgive him for the pain he'd caused. He was thankful he had been able to arrange his finances so that Sadie was able to attend Wooster. It had been tight, but his mom had insisted on paying for her books and other fees. Sadie had gotten a part time job. She was a good kid, never complaining. He prayed he'd be in a position to send her back the next year. He regretted he was unable to put Trey in the private school he and Samantha had discussed. Trey would have benefited a great deal from the smaller classes and more individual attention. Cynthia had the money, but Grant would never ask for her help. He had his dignity. It still stuck in his craw that this was her home. She reminded him of that at every opportunity. She was constantly bragging to guests that Roderick had built it especially for her. He was beginning to feel like a charity case or, worse, a kept man. He had an image to protect, he surely didn't want people to start thinking he was some kind of gigolo.

He needed to get the country house on the market. There was no use keeping it. He was certain Cynthia would not want to spend quiet weekends and summer vacations there. "She might miss a party," he thought sarcastically.

"Grant, aren't you ready yet? I don't want to be late. We've already missed most of the cocktail hour. I told you this is a sit down dinner. I hope you aren't trying to embarrass me."

"I'm ready, just relax. We'll be there in plenty of time. No one ever starts these things on time."

The evening was pleasant, but Grant could not enjoy it for thinking of what he should be doing for his case tomorrow. Cynthia was surrounded by several of the local politicians. She was in her element. He knew she was going to be angry, but he needed to leave. Catching her eye across the room, he motioned toward the door. Her annoyance was immediate. She continued to talk hoping he would change his mind if she ignored him. Grant was not to be put off. Walking to her side, he took her elbow. Smiling he said, "Sorry to have to break up the party, gentlemen, but Cynthia and I must say goodnight. I have an early court session. Come along, dear, we must thank our hosts."

The ride home that night was silent. The tension was like a thick fog surrounding them, suffocating them. Each was locked in their own thoughts. Grant was mentally reviewing his strategy for court, and Cynthia was fuming that Grant had dragged her away so early. She had never realized the advantage she'd had being married to older men. They had made their money, gotten their kicks by outdoing their opponents, and were ready to dote on her. They could show her the attention she deserved. She had always been center stage. "I sure as hell don't plan to change now." The resentful thought was so strong it was almost audible. What made her think she needed a young, virile husband anyway? She'd rather not be married, but she needed the respectability it allowed and the protection in case of anything unexpected. Despite all her worldliness, Cynthia wasn't sure she could handle abortion.

"Grant was a mistake," she thought. "I should have married an older man and found a young lover." She didn't like sharing Grant with a career and those kids of his. Every time she thought they might take a short trip, Grant couldn't go because Trey had a swim meet, basketball game, or tennis tournament. She was sick of the kid hanging around the house. It destroyed her spontaneity. She liked parading around in the buff, teasing Grant. She had a sensuous body and she damn well wanted to flaunt it. She liked to get him aroused when she knew they couldn't follow through immediately. She loved to watch him squirm. His discomfort was a turn on for her. She loved the power she wielded in those situations. She resented not having the freedom to prove to Grant she still controlled him. She had been uptight about it. She felt herself losing control. She no longer had the upper hand. She would change her tactics. Grant never put her first anymore, and she would not tolerate that. If he weren't man enough to handle his career and her, then she'd have to do something about the situation. She wasn't going to live that way. Maybe she could suggest that Trey needed to spend a little more time with his mother. She was sure Samantha didn't have a life and would be delighted to have him with her. Setting her jaw, she vowed she'd mold Grant to her image or he'd be out of here. No one was going to make her unhappy. She had battled too hard and waited too long to not enjoy the spoils. She'd just eliminate Grant from her life if he couldn't see things her way, but he sure as hell wasn't taking any of her money with him. After all, there were plenty of other fish in the sea, and lately several had subtly and some not so subtly indicated their interest.

Chapter 17

Samantha was restless tonight. She should have made plans to go to a movie or out to dinner, but she hated doing things alone. All her friends were married so she disliked taking them away from their families evenings and weekends. Besides many of them didn't seem to have time for her now that she was divorced. "The old 'watch out for that divorcee' syndrome," she thought ruefully. Maybe a long hot bath would make her feel better. Her bathroom was one of the most peaceful rooms in the house. She had insisted it be very large. It was decorated with varying shades of white, cream, and a touch of sea foam green. Several baskets of ivy adorned the ledge in front of an arched floor to ceiling window overlooking a beautiful and tranquil garden. She had worked with a landscaper to incorporate the use of the ancient Eastern theory of Feng Shui to create peace and harmony. She was definitely a believer. Gazing out into it was like a sedative. She always walked away with her mind clear and her body relaxed. She lit several candles and turned on soft music before stepping into the oversized marble tub. She clicked on the Jacuzzi and let the water caress her skin while her eyes strolled through the garden. She sensed the fragrant flowers, smelled the fresh night air, and felt the texture of the foliage and the allure of the silent and majestic sculptures. She felt better already. She laid back and let her senses enjoy the moment.

She emerged later renewed. Feeling like a new woman, she donned her favorite silk pajamas and headed downstairs. She selected an Eric Clapton CD, poured a glass of wine, and stretched out to do some soul searching. Her life had no direction, it was just pulling her along. She needed to make some decisions. What did she want to do? She knew she had to get her life back on track, start again, but where did that take her? Ever since she had run into Peter Stanton at the Terrace Room he had been on her mind. She knew there was a mutual attraction. She was sure they had both felt it while she was decorating his home. They had talked so comfortably, laughed so easily. It had felt so good, too good at the time. Samantha felt the tension building. She didn't want to be hurt again. She had felt that way with Grant and look what happened. She couldn't let that happen again. She couldn't survive another hurt like that. She was too vulnerable.

"If Peter calls, I'll find an excuse. I just couldn't risk it. It would be nice to talk to him though. He always makes me feel so good, so important, almost special," she said aloud as if to reaffirm her feelings.

She couldn't remember the last time she really felt special. He was a very sensitive and caring man. She had observed how he had treated his housekeeper, Betsy, and the gardener. They had never talked about family. She wondered if he had ever been married or had children. Funny how you can feel close to someone but still not know anything about them. She liked him but knew very little about his personal life. Abruptly she stopped, what did it matter, she wasn't going to get close to anyone again.

~~~~~~~~~~~~~~~~

Samantha woke and stretched lazily. It was Saturday, but Trey was not coming over this weekend, so she could take her time moving around. She loved mornings like this when she could just follow her whims. She rarely ate breakfast, but today she was ravenous. Fresh blueberry muffins sounded wonderful. She could almost smell them baking. She could have them in the oven in a matter of minutes. She would grind that special blend of Sumatran and Kenyan coffee beans she had picked up at the mall yesterday. She liked the bite of the Sumatran and the rich flavor of the Kenyan. She would even indulge in real butter. She could afford the calories. Her mouth watered just thinking about it. She stopped by the den to start a fire in the fireplace. There was something so cozy and therapeutic about those flickering flames. Moving into the kitchen she swung into motion while humming off key. The smell from the fresh coffee beans was intoxicating. Coffee was her addiction. She'd never smoked, and only occasionally had a glass of wine, but her coffee was a must. After whipping up the muffins and popping them into the oven, she retreated to the den. Settling into her favorite recliner, she leaned back to gaze at the fire only to chuckle as her eyes focused on her feet. Staring back at her from her feet were two, huge, gray, fuzzy mice with little white ears, pink noses, and dark beady eyes. She kicked her foot in the air to see a long tail dangling from the back of her heel. Trey had given them to her several Christmases ago. They had enjoyed great fun with them. She loved them and the memories they brought.

Samantha leaned back. Maybe she could make a new life after all. She still had her memories, and no one could take that away from her. There were a lot of things she had wanted to do, but she had never had the time. She had already decided she was going to limit the time she devoted to community work. She no longer had to support Grant's image in the community. She had already enrolled in a sculpting class for the summer. Yesterday, she read an advertisement for yoga classes and planned to check into it. She was even thinking of learning to ski. She had always wanted to try her skill on the slopes. That would require some traveling since there were no ski resorts in the area. She had grown up water skiing but had never tried snow skiing. Her travel agent could probably recommend a good resort. She might be able to join a group tour. All of her friends were married with families, so they weren't free to go with her. It would definitely be wise to develop a circle of single friends. She wasn't exactly sure how to do that. She didn't like to go to bars. For the first time in years, she had many choices. Excitement began to build as she contemplated her future.

The oven timer brought her back to reality. The smell of freshly baked muffins and the aroma of coffee filled the air. Samantha felt good. She knew she had made it over another hurdle. Consciously, she had reached the important decision to move forward with her life. She felt the excitement grow.

"I can do this," she affirmed. "I will do this." With a contented smile, she padded back to the den to enjoy the first breakfast of her new life in front of the warm hearth.

~~~~~~~~~~~~~~~~~

Margaret called on Wednesday to say she had been in a baking mood, and she was bringing Samantha her favorite, a coconut cream pie. Samantha knew Margaret loved to bake but she sensed a hidden agenda to the visit. When she arrived carrying a delectable looking pie, Samantha offered to make coffee and they sat in the kitchen for a cozy chat. They laughed and talked awhile, then Samantha noticed the crease appear in Margaret's brow.

"Is something bothering you, Margaret?"

Margaret sighed, "I'm not sure, really. I had dinner last night with Grant, Trey, and Cynthia. She has Trey waiting on her hand and foot. 'Trey, get me this! Trey, get me that!' Why she treats him like he's hired help. Of course, he doesn't complain because he wants to make his dad happy. But then she treats everyone like a servant. I swear before that evening was over, she even asked me to bring her another cup of tea. Now, Samantha, you know I'm not lazy, but I was guest in *that* woman's house. Grant tried to smooth it over, but I know it embarrassed him. I hope he hasn't made a mistake."

Samantha tried to ease Margaret's mind by reassuring her that things would work out. Secretly, she wondered if all was not well in wonderland? "Maybe the Queen of Hearts will beat her to death with her wand," Samantha fantasized. With a malicious smile, she envisioned Cynthia being buffeted by an angry queen holding a huge heart on the end of a club.

Chapter 18

Cynthia opened the door and walked into a dark cloud of smoke. The bar smelled of beer and vomit and sweaty bodies. Cynthia fought down the feeling of revulsion. The loud jukebox music crashed into her eardrums as the television sportscaster shouted plays over the dull roar of conversation.

Cynthia wasn't comfortable in this sleazy bar atmosphere, but she had heard that Freddie hung out here. She had tried to find a phone number but he evidently was unlisted. Freddie and Cynthia had been close in high school, real close, but that was before she became Mrs. Buckingham White. Buckingham had been Cynthia's first husband. He was thirty years her senior and very wealthy. Cynthia had endured the May-September jokes from her family, the disapproving stares from Buck's sisters, and outright insults from his children. Cynthia was a little bitter about her marriage to Buck. She had put up with that old buzzard for four years before he finally had the courtesy to kick the bucket. He was in declining health for two years before he succumbed to a heart attack. Cynthia had inherited a small amount of money from Buck, but she had expected a lot more. He had assured her that he loved her more than life itself and was leaving her well fixed. What he left her was just enough to keep her in expensive clothes, apartment, and car until she found Roderick Barker. Buck hadn't even left her the house. He'd left that to his children. Cynthia got only what was in their pre-nuptial agreement. If she'd known he was going to be so stingy, she would have held out for more before she married him. He wanted her badly. She was beautiful and he needed to prove to the world that he was man enough to handle a young woman. He would have agreed to a lot more.

"This is just to satisfy the lawyer," he had said. "I'll leave you a substantial amount in my will." He had become really stingy after his health started to decline. He had questioned her about all the credit cards, every little purchase. She thought his family had turned him against her. That sniveling, fat ass, Virginia, hadn't smiled at Cynthia once in the four years Cynthia was married to her brother. Cynthia had tried hard to win them over. She needed their support. It was to no avail, she was selling, but they weren't buying.

Cynthia looked around. She felt uneasy in this place. She saw several men eying her eagerly from the bar. She decided to pass up the bar and take a booth in a dark corner from which she could observe the comings and goings in the bar. She had a good view of the door. If Freddie came in she would be able to spot him right away. Cynthia had no doubt he would recognize her. After the time they spent together she felt she was indelibly imprinted upon his brain, not to mention upon his body.

"Oh, no," thought Cynthia, as a strapping young fellow in his twenties started toward the booth.

He bent down over Cynthia. "Can I buy you a drink?" he asked as he started to slide in beside Cynthia.

"You can't sit here."

"Why not, honey, you look like you could use some company, and I'm kind of partial to older women." That stung and Cynthia reacted angrily.

"Get out of my booth. I don't want your company."

"What's the matter, bitch, I'm not uptown enough for you? What are you doing down here anyway?" He snarled.

Suddenly the light was blotted from the booth. A soft voice said, "Punk, I believe you're in my seat." Cynthia looked up to see an older, but still slick-looking Freddie. Relief flooded over her.

"Thank God, you're here," she said to Freddie. The young man rose quietly and melted away. He obviously knew Freddie and respected him, or was it fear? Cynthia couldn't tell because his face had become inscrutable when Freddie showed up.

"I'm here," Freddie said, "but the question is why are you?"

"I was looking for you."

Freddie grinned, "I figured that, but why?" He leered, "Want to rehash old times or better still replay them?"

"I was thinking of you, Freddie, I heard you had been…ah…away."

Freddie laughed, "You can say it, doll. Everyone here knows I've done time and they know why."

"Did you really kill those two men?"

Freddie looked at her, "It was self defense." Then he smiled and slowly winked at her. That gesture conveyed more information than any words he might have spoken. "You haven't told me why you're here," Freddie was serious and his manner was very cool now. Cynthia shivered involuntarily. "Are you cold? We can take a walk in the sunlight," Freddie suggested. He was not totally without feeling, and he knew this was not the environment in which she would be comfortable. It hadn't been even back when her circumstances were not so good. Freddie couldn't remember the number of times he had stolen money so he could take her to some fancy joint. It was either that or not enjoy her favors. Freddie was a realist, however. He knew Cynthia had not sought him out for his company. She wanted something. But what?

Jack Reed noticed Cynthia the moment she arrived at the bar. "What the hell is Grant's wife doing in a place like this," he speculated. It wasn't unusual for Jack to be here. Many of his clients and witnesses came from this part of town. He had long since decided that the Riverside Bar made a good satellite office.

His clients were comfortable here; but he just couldn't see the sophisticated, haughty Cynthia hanging out here.

Jack watched as a young man approached her. "Well, I'll be damned," he muttered softly as he saw Freddie Franklin walk over and eject the young man from the booth. "Now, what business could she have with Freddie?" Jack started at the sound of his voice. He was so astonished that he had spoken aloud. He continued to watch as the two left the bar. "Looks like old Grant is being cuckolded," he grinned.

"I hear you've married again," Freddie said as he steered Cynthia out into the blinding light of day. He slipped on sunglasses. Cynthia had to dig around in her purse. Unlike Freddie, she wasn't accustomed to coming from dark bars into blazing sunlight so she wasn't prepared. "Let's walk by the river," Freddie suggested. "We won't be overheard there." Whatever she wanted from him he knew she would want it to be private...very private. A flood of nostalgia rushed over Freddie. He wished..."Forget it. It was never really like that," Freddie admonished himself. He had at one time entertained thoughts of making their relationship permanent. Cynthia had disavowed him of that notion posthaste.

"The river is really beautiful at this time of year," Cynthia ventured.

"Yeah," he responded. There was a long silence. Freddie decided to let her make the first move.

"I've heard rumors that you could help a person," timidly.

"Depends on what's needed," he responded laconically.

"Well, if someone wanted to alter a situation."

"You mean change things. In what way?"

"Well...if someone wanted to get rid of some...something."

"Something? Or someone?" Freddie was no fool. He quickly saw where this going. "The someone, your husband?"

"He's very cruel to me, Freddie."

"Yeah, and how much will you inherit? I hear you did all right when old Barker kicked the bucket."

"That's not it at all, Freddie. If something isn't done, I'm going to go crazy. He's driving me insane."

"How much?"

Cynthia hesitated, "He has a million dollar life insurance policy."

"You the beneficiary?"

"Yes."

"What else?"

"What do you mean, what else?"

"You know very well what I mean. What else will you get?"

"He has a successful law practice. But he has to pay alimony and child support. He has a house in the country. Other than that I don't think his finances are very good."

Freddie stopped and turned Cynthia to face him. "What are you proposing here, Cynthia?"

"You know what I'm asking."

That wasn't good enough for Freddie. If he was going to consider this, he had to make her say the words. She had to fully implicate herself, then she would never be able to throw him to the wolves. "No, I'm not sure I do."

"I want to get rid of my husband."

Not good enough. She had to say the words. "If you want rid of him, you can just leave, just divorce him. That's simple enough."

"I can't divorce him. In the last two years I've made a number of successful investments on Grant's advice, but I used my money. I'm not going to give him half of my returns. Freddie, why are you being so dense?"

"Am I being dense? Then why don't you tell me exactly what you want."

"I want you to kill Grant," Cynthia belched the words out in a manner reminiscent of cleansing a sour stomach.

Freddie smiled, "Was that so hard?"

Cynthia glared at him. He was so insolent. That was the thing she had hated about him in high school, but, man, she had loved his body. At the memory she felt a warm tingling sensation in her groin. "Get a grip, Cynthia," she thought. "This guy is a sleaze ball murderer." The thought brought another rush of sensation. He excited her. He always had. He just didn't fit into her plans. For one thing he didn't think big enough. He would always be penny ante, pulling small cons and pulling someone else's trigger.

"Cynthia, are you listening to me?" Freddie's voice jerked her back. "Good grief, where were you? I asked you three times."

Cynthia flushed, "I'm sorry, what did you ask?"

"What's in it for me if I help you with this little problem?"

"Ten thousand."

"You must be joking. I wouldn't get out of bed for that."

Cynthia realized that she had misjudged his financial requirements.

"Twenty," she said quickly.

"Half a mil."

"No way," Cynthia said, "a hundred."

"Two hundred, half of it up front." Cynthia nodded in agreement.

Freddie felt a little sadistic. "Say it. 'I'll pay you two hundred thousand dollars to kill my husband.'"

Cynthia flushed. She remembered this side of him with no pleasure. Gritting her teeth she repeated the statement. She wasn't stupid. She knew he was forcing her to irrevocably implicate herself.

"Okay, when do you want it done."

"Soon, and it has to look like an accident."

"Got one of those double indemnity policies?"

"Yes, it has to be an accident…or natural causes."

Freddie began walking back toward the bar.

"Will you do it?" Cynthia felt panicky.

"I'll think about how and if it can be done. Meet me here next Thursday."

"At the bar?"

"No," Freddie felt slightly irritated. "Here on the riverside. We can't be seen together. I'll need to know all about your husband. Where he goes, what he does, who he sees, what he drives, the hours he keeps, etc., etc., etc."

"Can't we do that now?" Cynthia pleaded. She wanted this over as quickly as possible.

"Nah, I have another appointment waiting for me at the bar. Figured he could wait while I enjoyed your company."

"What time on Thursday?"

"Eleven o'clock."

"Oh, I can't come at eleven. I have an hair appointment."

Freddie looked at her with raised eyebrows, "You want to do this or not?"

"I'll change my appointment."

"I guess so," Freddie retorted. "See ya." He strode off leaving her slightly scared and feeling very small.

Chapter 19

Margaret slowly turned into the driveway. She didn't see the car parked slightly down the block or the man with narrowed eyes watching her. She disliked going to Cynthia's house. It clearly was Cynthia's house and not her son's. Cynthia took every opportunity to remind her of the fact. It was too palatial, too formal, all marble with crystal chandeliers, huge urns and vases. The walls were adorned with gilded mirrors and ornate picture frames. It was cold. It reminded Margaret of a museum. Even the furnishings were stiff and uncomfortable chosen for appearance rather than practicality. Expensive, yes, but it had no warmth. It was hard to believe anyone lived here. She didn't know how Grant could tolerate it. He had been raised in elegant but comfortable and inviting surroundings. What was Cynthia doing to him? Margaret didn't like Cynthia and with good cause. Her son's new wife, and that's the way Margaret always thought of her, his new wife treated her with no respect at all. Not only did Cynthia order Margaret around in her house; she took the same attitude in Margaret's home. Unfortunately, or fortunately, depending upon one's perspective, Cynthia and Grant rarely visited Margaret and Forest so if they were to see their son, they had to go to Cynthia's house.

Freddie watched the older woman park and walk around the side of Cynthia's house. A housekeeper, maybe? No, Freddie decided. She was driving too nice of a car. Housekeepers didn't drive Cadillacs. It wasn't Cynthia's mother. She was dead. Maybe a friend or relative. It had to be someone Cynthia knew well, otherwise, the woman would have gone to the front door. Freddie noted that the back entrance was around the right side of the house. Wouldn't be too hard to slip into a big place like that. Big houses were always easier than small ones. Less likelihood of being heard. Freddie put the car in gear and moved down the street. He wanted to learn more before he made his move but it wouldn't be good for his car to be noticed. He would have to leave it a street or two away. Freddie thoughts returned to the older woman. He didn't like not knowing who and where everyone was.

Mildred opened the door to Margaret.
"Come in, Mrs. James."
"Hello, Mildred, how are you?"
"I'm fine, Ma'am. I'll tell Miss Cynthia you are here."
Margaret could hear the annoyance in Cynthia's voice.
"She's finally here! The other guests will be arriving anytime. She needs to make the salad, Mildred. I'll be out directly."

Mildred looked embarrassed as she returned. "Ma'am, she says you should make the salad. She's running a little behind."

"It's okay, Mildred, don't let it trouble you."

Mildred flashed her a grateful glance. Margaret stepped into the kitchen, greeted the cook, and took out the salad utensils. Margaret spent more time in Cynthia's kitchen than she did her own. She never understood why Cynthia's cook couldn't make the salad when she had parties. Margaret suspected it was a control maneuver. Cynthia was a very controlling person.

Margaret's mind flashed back to the first time Grant had brought Cynthia to meet them. She had barely seated them when Cynthia said, "Could I, please, have a cup of herbal tea, dear." Margaret had been somewhat taken aback and shocked at the rudeness and was further amazed to find Cynthia carried her own sweetener. As soon as she had finished greeting them, Margaret would have offered a beverage. She attributed the incident to Cynthia's being nervous. She now knew that had been Cynthia's way of establishing from the very beginning who was in control. Forest thought she was imagining it, but she had seen through this woman.

"Margaret, the guests will be here soon and you haven't started the salad." Margaret jerked when she heard Cynthia's strident voice.

"I'm really sorry," she mumbled. "I had to run a few errands before I came." Margaret hated herself when she felt intimidated by Cynthia. No one, but no one, had ever before made her feel intimidated. She hated the feeling and she hated Cynthia. How had she let this woman begin expecting her to always prepare her salads for dinner? Each time Margaret vowed to never do it again and then she did. Margaret laughed bitterly. After dinner it would be, "Margaret, dear, will you make the tea while I take our guests into the living room." Cynthia insisted upon serving tea after dinner although most of her guests would have preferred coffee. Margaret had thought more than once of dumping a half bottle of Tabasco into Cynthia's tea. She had restrained herself for Grant's sake.

Grant was upset upon finding his mother in the kitchen preparing salad for dinner.

"Mom, why are you doing this? We have a cook."

"Cynthia prefers that I do the salads."

"I'll speak to her, Mom, I don't want you in the kitchen preparing food when you visit us." Then he spoke angrily, "I don't know what is wrong with that woman. She doesn't treat you with respect. She doesn't respect me or anyone else for that matter. She's just all about herself."

Margaret put her hand on Grant's shoulder. "You're not very happy, are you, Son?" Grant shook his head. "Why did you leave Samantha and your children, Grant? You always seemed so happy."

Chapter 20

Everyday since she decided to move forward with her life, Samantha started each morning with a renewed sense of direction. She eagerly anticipated her sculpting classes, and she seemed to have a natural talent for it. When her fingers touched the clay, it communicated her moods and thoughts. The clay subject took on a personality without her consciously planning it. She was anxious to develop her own style. Presently, her instructor was assigning projects so that the students could gain overall skills and experience different techniques. Samantha looked forward to the time when she felt inspired and could let her creative juices flow. Working the clay was wonderful therapy. She could get lost in it for hours without thinking of anything else. Sometimes she went all day without eating. It took something very interesting to make her forget to eat. Maybe sculpting was the revolutionary new diet for her life. Samantha enjoyed the other students in her class. Their ages varied from teens to seventies, a very diverse group with a friendly camaraderie. Sculpting was probably their only common interest.

Samantha realized she had spent almost an hour daydreaming over her morning coffee. Checking her watch, she swung into action. She was meeting a client for lunch and then heading for a conference with her carpet supplier. Her business had suddenly picked up. Lately, Peter Stanton had referred several clients. The most recent was a vice-president of the local bank. She let her thoughts drift to Peter. He certainly popped into her mind often. What a gorgeous man he was. Well, she couldn't float around on that cloud or she would be late for her appointment. Shaking her head to clear it, she stepped into the shower. She chided herself, "Only room for one in here, you love struck, overgrown teenager. Maybe, I should make this a cold shower."

Randy Marshal was waiting in the lobby when Samantha arrived. Apologizing for her tardiness, she introduced herself. She requested the maitre d' seat them where they had privacy to discuss business. She wanted to present her ideas with minimal distractions. Little did she know she already had Randy's undivided attention. He had seen Peter's house, so he knew she did outstanding work. Peter spoke highly of her creativity and attention to detail. What he had failed to tell Randy was that she was also great on the eyes. Now, he knew why Peter had casually dropped a hint that she be invited to the barbecue Randy and his wife, Trudi, were planning for Saturday night. He must say the sneaky devil had excellent taste. Randy hadn't played matchmaker since college, but this might be very interesting.

Randy loved her ideas. His office was a dreary place. He always left each day feeling weary. He looked forward to a bright, cheery environment, which

She Loved Him

"We were until my investments went sour," he paused, "and then came along." He sounded bitter.

"Why don't you just leave her and go back to Samantha."

"It's too late for that. For one thing, Samantha wouldn't have me back

"Oh, Son, I know for a fact that she would take you back in a minute."

Cynthia stuck her head in the door and called. "Grant, our gues arriving. Don't be hanging around in the kitchen. Come out at once."

The man watching from the shadows faded back into the darkness. conversation had filled in the gaps. Now he not only knew who the older w was but he knew why Cynthia was in such a hurry.

Grant rolled his eyes at his mother and left the kitchen. Margaret h Forest come in. He had come directly from work. They owned one of the f furniture stores in town. They had an excellent manager, but Forest still ref to retire. He always said he would miss the people. He still got a thrill w making a sale. She was okay with his working as long as his health was go He was careful not to overstress himself; although he did have a heart probl which he controlled with medication. As a matter of fact, Margaret had a full time job keeping up with his medication. He was constantly misplacing it.

Margaret was disgusted as she heard her husband responding to Cynthia's flattery.

"Forest, you are looking terrific. Ladies, watch out tonight."

"You don't look too shabby yourself, Cynthia," he laughed.

Forest James was a handsome man. He stood over six feet and kept fit by staying active. He was tanned from his weekends of fishing. The deep tan was a striking contrast to his still blond hair. Margaret's heart smiled as she looked at him despite her annoyance with his obvious response to Cynthia's flirting.

Margaret made it through the evening and, just as she had predicted, she had been asked not only to make the tea, but also to serve it. Margaret left vowing never to return and knowing with dead certainty that she would. Forest didn't see it. Why were men so blind sometimes? Margaret was very tired of Cynthia, but she couldn't stop visiting her son.

still projected a calming atmosphere. His job was stressful enough without the décor adding to it. Peter had mentioned that she used Feng Shui and color therapy in her decorating. Randy was intrigued and hoped her techniques were successful.

They agreed on a starting date. Randy gave her authority to make all the selections. Samantha was flattered by his confidence. Before leaving, Randy had convinced her to attend his barbecue. He told her it would be an opportunity to get to know his tastes. She had thought this was a good idea. It would also give her an opportunity to expand her social circle. He failed to mention that Peter would be there. He'd let that devil figure out his own strategy. He was going to enjoy watching his confirmed bachelor friend clip his own wings. He had a feeling about this one. She was classy, witty, and intelligent. She was beautiful with a freshness he couldn't define. Peter Stanton may have just met his destiny head on. Randy could hardly wait for Saturday to observe this event unfold.

Samantha was surprised when Peter called on Friday offering to drive her to Randy and Trudi's barbecue. She didn't know why it had not occurred to her that he would be there. After all, he was the one who referred Randy to her. Once again she felt the pull of attraction and reminded herself not to get involved. She had no intention of being hurt again. If she allowed herself to care, she'd risk heartbreak. The only way to prevent that was to keep her distance. However, it would be rude to refuse his offer to give her a ride. After all, he wasn't asking her for a date. It was just a kind gesture. He was an important client and was sending her a lot of business. "I certainly can't afford to offend him," she rationalized.

Samantha was as breathless as a teenager on a first date when she answered the door Saturday evening. Peter was the picture of casual elegance. He was dressed in khaki slacks, soft sage green knit Ralph Lauren Polo shirt, and tasseled brown loafers. The twinkle in his eyes and that engaging lopsided grin made her heart skip a couple of beats. "Hi, Peter, please, come in. I'll only be a moment. Can I make you a drink?" She hoped he couldn't tell how flustered she was.

"Well, hello to you. You look lovely tonight. I'll pass on the drink, but thank you." Silently he told himself, "I'll just drink in your beauty. You are intoxicating enough to make me lightheaded." His emotions had a way of racing out of control when she was around. She always looked like she had stepped out of a fashion magazine. Her ecru linen slacks and matching shirt were very simple, accented only with a brown woven leather belt and soft leather sandals. Her skin was lightly tanned giving her a golden glow. She wore small, wooden, looped earrings and a tiny gold pendant around her neck. He noticed she wore no adornments on her arms or hands. Her aura was one of youthful freshness. He loved the simplicity of her beauty. This woman could easily steal his heart. The thought pleased him. Samantha offered him a seat while she returned to her bedroom to put the finishing touches on her hair. She realized her hands were trembling. This man brought unwanted and unexpected responses to Samantha that had been long forgotten. She would really have to keep her guard up to establish and maintain a casual friendship with Peter.

It was a very pleasant evening. Samantha found her eyes unconsciously searching for Peter. Several times she found him studying her intently. It wasn't difficult to read those golden brown eyes. They sent the message loud and clear, "Desire!!" Her body responded with unbidden tremors stirring deep inside her. The sexual tension was electric between them. Samantha wasn't sure she could deny her physical attraction to this man, but she, also, wasn't sure she would be willing to risk another relationship. Could she have a physical relationship with Peter without giving him her heart? She was frozen with fear of the tremendous pain that could accompany such powerful feelings.

The ride to her house that night was silent. Each of them aware of the other but lost in their own private thoughts. Peter wrestled with how to make his move. He wanted to know her better. Hell, he wanted to know everything about her, to touch her, to kiss her, to caress her. He wanted to take her in his arms and never let her go. His emotions far surpassed the sexual attraction he felt. He wanted to possess, protect, and love her. He wanted to wake up with her next to him each morning for the rest of their lives. He'd always known that when the right girl came along, he'd know it. He didn't dare move too fast and scare her off. He had sensed her reluctance on several occasions. He had felt her withdraw emotionally before. After all, she'd just been through a divorce. He didn't know the circumstances, but, at its best, divorce was painful and emotionally draining. He didn't want her on the rebound. He wanted her to come to him because she wanted to be with him as much as he wanted to be with her.

Samantha stared out at the shadowy glow cast by the streetlights. Her feelings were not clear-cut, but illusive and changing. Her thoughts raced as she tried to identify true feelings. She liked this man very much and wanted to further their relationship; but she wasn't convinced that she had the strength to survive in the event he didn't share her feelings. Grant's betrayal had left her deeply scarred. She wanted to love again, but she was terribly afraid.

Peter stopped in her driveway jarring her back. He draped his arm around her as they approached the door. He turned her gently to face him. His eyes were pools of tenderness.

"Samantha, I hope this is not rushing you, but I want very much to see you again. I could have my housekeeper pack a picnic lunch and bottle of wine," he hurried on before she could say no. "We could find a quiet spot and enjoy the sailboats on Lake Loma tomorrow. What do you think?" He held his breath fearing she would refuse his offer.

Samantha was overwhelmed with emotion, a mixture of elation and bone chilling fear. She bit her lip and stared into those golden eyes that seemed to look into her soul. With a jolt, she felt the connection and heard her voice responding. "I'd like that very much."

She heard Peter's quick intake of breath. He took her chin in his hand and lifted her head. She knew he was going to kiss her. Their eyes locked. She wasn't sure who moved first. They were wrapped in a passionate, almost frantic embrace tasting the nectar of their need. Their passion ignited a depth of feeling that neither expected, and it threatened to overwhelm them. Peter pulled away, reluctantly, remembering his vow not to move too quickly. Only the night's sounds surrounded them as they stood in silent embrace. Peter planted gentle kisses on her temple and hair, basking in her scent. He was too moved to speak. Samantha's throat was tight with emotion. She had not anticipated this effect.

"It's late, Peter, I think I'd better go in. What time is the picnic tomorrow?"

Peter cleared his throat, hoping he could find his voice. "How about one-thirty, pretty lady?" Samantha nodded and quietly opened the door. Peter flashed her a dazzling smile, turned, and strode to his car. He was already counting the hours until he could see her again.

Samantha leaned against the door with a sigh. She didn't know what the future held, but she'd made her decision. There was no turning back now. Peter might very well devour her, heart and soul, but she could only hope the feeling was mutual.

Chapter 21

As Margaret braked her car in front of Grant's house, she felt something tap the side of her foot. Reaching down, she felt a small vial. "Forest's medicine," she thought. It must have fallen from his pocket when he borrowed her car last week. Dr. Sims had given him a sound scolding when Forest had asked for a replacement prescription. Margaret smiled as she remembered her husband grumbling about "young doctors not dry behind the ears lecturing you about being careless." She dropped the vial into her pocket and hurried into the house. Forest was not going to join them tonight for dinner. He had told Margaret that he'd had his dose of Cynthia earlier in the week, when she called to ask if he could give her a hand with a community project, and then left him to complete the whole job. Margaret wondered if he was beginning to understand her dislike for Cynthia.

Margaret was surprised to find Cynthia in the kitchen making a cup of tea. She generally had her tea after dinner rather than before. "At which time she asks me to make it," thought Margaret wryly. Just then the phone rang. "I'll be right back," Cynthia said, "I've been expecting a call." She left the room.

Curious, since there was a phone in the kitchen, Margaret stepped to the door. She could hear Cynthia's voice but the words were muffled. She didn't see the gardener quietly pass through the room behind her. She was straining to hear the voice beyond the door. Cynthia's tone was strident, but that was not unusual for Cynthia. Margaret heard her say, "I'll be there in ten minutes. Don't keep me waiting. I have guests here for dinner."

Margaret reflected back over the last several weeks. It just wasn't right the way Cynthia was making everyone's life a misery. Samantha was trying to build a new life, but Margaret knew that she still loved and missed Grant. Trey had come to live with his father, but Margaret could tell he wasn't happy. Sadie was away at college. What had been a loving, close-knit family was now separated. "Cynthia is responsible for totally destroying a happy family," Margaret thought bitterly. She sighed in resignation and turned back to the kitchen. Margaret looked at the cup of tea and considered taking it to Cynthia, but decided to begin the salad instead.

Cynthia dropped the phone in the cradle and returned to the kitchen. She picked up the tea and turned to Margaret. "Grant will be here soon. You are going to make the salad, aren't you dear?" She smiled but her tone negated any positive affect turning the request into a command. Margaret had already begun the salad making and chose to ignore her remark. Cynthia clearly did not expect a response. She walked into the living room and sat down in Grant's chair, placing the cup of tea on the side table. She took a sip and grimaced. "Good heavens, this tea is as weak as water and tastes terrible," she muttered. "That's a blend I won't buy again." She set the cup back on the saucer. She reached in her pocket, took out a small vial, and emptied it into the tea. When she heard Grant in the foyer, she picked up her purse and headed for the door.

"Where are you going?" he asked, surprised that she was leaving at dinnertime. He knew his mother was here. He had seen her car around the side. "I've a quick errand to run. I'll be right back." Cynthia's voice was terse. She paused and added, "I made a cup of tea for you. It's on the table by your chair." Grant gave her a sharp look but inquired no further. He picked up the mail and began to sort through it. He stood there a few minutes before he walked over and lifted the cup of tea. He felt and it was still warm. He was sure his mother had made it for Cynthia. He knew Cynthia did not make the tea for him. Cynthia was such an ungrateful, thoughtless bitch to have walked off and left it untouched. He wouldn't have his mother offended by Cynthia's rudeness, so he tipped it up and drained it before going into the kitchen to greet his mother. If this was one of Cynthia's new blends, he'd have to tell her he didn't care for this latest one. He really wasn't an expert on tea. He drank it when Cynthia served it, but his real preference was coffee.

"Hi, Mom," Grant hugged his mother. "What's cooking?" This time he addressed the cook.

"Your favorite, Mr. James. Your mother planned the menu tonight."

"Figures." Grant walked around the kitchen sampling anything available until his mother playfully smacked his hand with a spoon.

Grant grinned and went back into the living room. He suddenly felt a little dizzy. He sat down on the edge of the sofa. He felt like someone had a vise around his chest squeezing. His breathing became ragged and forced. "What is happening?" He whispered. He tried to lie over on the sofa and fell to the floor just as Trey walked in.

"Dad, what's wrong?" Trey cried in alarm. "Hey, somebody, there's something wrong with Dad." Margaret and the cook ran in just as Mildred came from the other end of the house.

Margaret knelt by Grant. "Call 911. He's unconscious."

Mildred sounded far away when she asked, "Is he breathing? Ma'am, they want to know if he's breathing."

"This can't be happening," thought Margaret.

"Mrs. James, is he breathing?"

Trey pushed his grandmother out of the way and checked. "Yes, he's breathing," he replied.

"He's breathing," Mildred repeated into the phone. "Yes, I'll stay on the line."

Cynthia appeared at the door. "What is going on here?" she asked harshly, then she spotted Grant. "What's wrong with Grant? What's happened?" She knelt beside Trey.

"We don't know. He just fell to the floor. We called 911. They're on the way," Trey explained. Margaret, unable to comprehend what was happening, looked at Cynthia. Sirens screamed into the driveway and Trey ran to open the door. Three EMT's rushed into the room. Two began working on Grant while the third, a girl who looked as young as Trey, began asking questions.

Margaret heard the EMT's say they were having trouble stabilizing him. She knew they were preparing to transport Grant to the hospital. She struggled to stand up and follow. Losing her balance she stumbled and grabbed for the side table sending the empty cup and saucer crashing to the floor. She stared blankly at the broken china and then raised her eyes to Cynthia with a dazed expression. Her shoulders shook as she sobbed. "Oh, no! Oh, no! Not my Grant, not my Grant."

Trey was immediately beside his grandmother, leading her to a chair. He was frightened but he thought, "I've got to be strong for Grandmother."

"You'd better call Grandfather," he said to Cynthia.

Cynthia was strangely calm. The EMT's would remember this. She picked up the phone and dialed, "Forest, there's a problem. It appears Grant's had a heart attack."

"No, I think you need to come here first. Margaret is distraught; she'll need your help to get to the hospital."

Trey knew he had to notify his mother. He dialed her number dreading what he must tell her. After several rings, her machine picked up. He had a sinking feeling. He knew she was not there. She didn't screen calls. He hung up. He would call again from the hospital.

The medics were moving Grant to the ambulance. Cynthia turned to Trey. "You'd better come with me."

"I can't leave Grandmother alone."

"Your father needs you now," Cynthia said sharply. "Mildred will stay with Margaret until Forest comes." Trey looked anxiously at his grandmother then at Mildred.

Mildred nodded woodenly. "There's too much death in this house," she thought sadly.

Three hours later Dr. Sims moved slowly toward the waiting room. His own heart felt heavy as he thought of his friend lying lifeless in the room behind him, and all those friends waiting for him down the hall trusting him to save this man they loved.

~~~~~~~~~~~~~~~~~

Samantha had an uneasy feeling. She wasn't sure what was precipitating such a mood. Normally, she didn't make evening appointments, but had made an exception tonight and now she was uncomfortable with that decision. She was anxious to get home. Earlier she had found it difficult not to be impatient with the Tucker's. It appeared that they could never agree on anything. Some couples thrived on conflict, but she tried to avoid that in her life. She hoped this job didn't turn out to be an unpleasant experience. Her intuition told her to complete this job quickly before they could change their minds.

Samantha closed the garage door and paused at the kitchen cabinet to check her calls. According to her caller ID, Grant's number was listed last. Trey had probably called. She'd get into something more comfortable before returning his call. As if some invisible hand pulled her back, Samantha whirled, dropped her purse and quickly punched in Trey's number.

Mildred answered, "James' residence."

"Mildred, it's Samantha. May I speak with Trey, please?"

After a long pause, Mildred replied, "Oh, Mrs. James, you haven't heard?"

"Heard what? Mildred, is there some problem with Trey?"

"No, Ma'am, the problem is with Mr. James."

"Grant?" Samantha froze.

"Yes, ma'am, it appears he has had a heart attack. They've taken him to the hospital."

Samantha was stunned. Surely she had misunderstood Mildred. "Mildred, are you saying Grant, Trey's father, had a heart attack?"

"Well, the EMTs thought that was the case. No one has called me back from the hospital to confirm it. They took him to Bryant Community Hospital since it was closest. You should probably just meet them there."

With heart pounding Samantha grabbed her purse and headed for the car. This couldn't be happening. Not to Grant. He was so healthy. There must be some mistake, but Mildred sounded certain.

Dashing into the emergency room Samantha spied Trey at the pay telephone booth. He hung up when he caught sight of her. "Oh! Mom, thank God, you're here. I've been trying to call you. It's Dad, they think he's had a heart attack." Samantha hugged her son, "Oh Trey, I'm so sorry. I'm sure he will be fine. Your dad is young and strong." She wished she felt as confident. As she and Trey started down the hallway, they saw Dr. Sims approach Cynthia, Margaret, and Forest. Her heart sank. She'd known Charlie Sims a long time and he wasn't smiling; in fact, he looked beaten. As if in slow motion she saw Cynthia stiffen and cover her mouth with her hand. Forest pulled a sobbing Margaret into his arms. His face was distorted with pain. Trey started running toward them. Samantha stood paralyzed momentarily, then dashed after Trey. Charlie turned to him. "Trey, I'm so, so sorry. I did everything I could, but it just wasn't enough." He acknowledged Samantha with a nod, turned and slowly retreated down the hall. Grant had been his friend. His shoulders slumped with the burden of the loss.

Trey turned to his mother, "Oh, Mom, what am I going to do without Dad? I love him so much. Why did this happen? Why my dad?" Samantha was at a loss for words. She just held him in stunned silence. They were both so torn by grief, words were not possible. Samantha was the first to speak. "I've got to call Sadie, but I don't want to call from here. Do you want to come home with me?" Trey nodded his consent, too overwhelmed to talk. "Let's go tell Grandfather and Grandmother, we'll be home if they need us."

Samantha moved forward. Ignoring Cynthia, she embraced Margaret and Forest expressing her sorrow. They knew how she felt. They knew she had never stopped loving Grant. "Trey and I will be at the house if you need us. Sadie has to be called. I think it would be better if I call from home. I want to try to locate her friend, Jamie, first. I don't want Sadie to be alone when I tell her. I'll call you later."

Driving home Samantha was lost in thought while Trey stared out the window not seeing anything. Samantha's heart was breaking not only for her children, but also for herself. She had lost Grant once and it had been painful. The loss she felt now was excruciating. She hurt for her children and their great loss. She understood their pain since she had lost her parents at a young age. Their death had created a void that had never been filled. Now the children had to deal with that same terrible emptiness. They had been so close to Grant. He had always been so much a part of their lives. Fate had certainly played a cruel trick.

~ ~ ~ ~ ~ ~ ~ ~ ~ ~ ~ ~ ~ ~ ~ ~

Calling Sadie had been one of the hardest things she had ever done. The anguish in Sadie's voice had torn at Samantha's heart. Words of comfort were not enough. She wanted to pull her into her arms, but circumstances didn't permit that. Samantha was so thankful she had been able to reach Jamie. Sadie and Jamie had become very close. She felt better knowing that Sadie had someone with her during those first bitter hours. Jamie had agreed to spend the night and drive Sadie to the airport in the morning. Tomorrow seemed a century away when her children needed her. Samantha turned off the light knowing little sleep would come this night.

Chapter 22

It was a cold, bleak day as they lowered Grant into the red clay hole. Samantha looked across the dead, brown, prairie grass doing battle with intermittent charges by an invisible army. This was really a terrible place where the children of nature constantly warred with the forces of nature. For the life of her she couldn't understand why Forest and Margaret had allowed Cynthia to choose this barren, forsaken spot to lay Grant to rest. Half the graves were totally neglected. Samantha could have understood if other family members had been buried here but they weren't. The Garden of Tranquility was fifteen miles out of town and was used mostly by farm families whose ancestors were interred here. It was as if Cynthia wanted him out of sight so he could easily be forgotten. Certainly no one would pass by his grave on the way to somewhere else. There was nothing out here except a few scattered farmhouses.

Samantha had to admit reluctantly that Cynthia had spared no expense on Grant's coffin. It was highly polished mahogany with solid brass hardware. On the other hand Cynthia had declined to have any flowers at the graveside service. The lack of flowers magnified the harshness of the day. Samantha's eyes swept over the small group lingering at the graveside. Cynthia stood with Margaret and Forest looking suitably grief-stricken in her neat, black, Christian Dior suit that plunged two inches below her cleavage line and ended six inches above her knees. "Displaying her wares for the next victim, no doubt," thought Samantha. Cynthia was not the kind of woman who lived alone for long. Samantha turned sharply and hurried from the grounds without saying goodbye to Margaret and Forest. Her children had declined to return to town in the family car and were waiting in her car. Samantha hadn't cried. She was still bitter and angry. The tears just wouldn't come, and dry grief was choking her. She had to escape from here and all those pitying glances.

~~~~~~~~~~~~~~~~

In the still of the night, with both children asleep, Samantha let her mind review the last seventy-two hours since learning of Grant's death. It had to be a nightmare. She still found it hard to believe Grant was dead. He had been the picture of health. She felt her body tensing. It just didn't add up. She let her thoughts flow unedited. Something wasn't right; she was sure of it. Her every instinct warned her. What should she do? She tossed and turned. Sleep evaded her. She went down to the kitchen and made some chamomile tea and stared out at the grey dawn. Maybe Jack Reed could help. She watched the clock while pacing the floor until she thought Jack would be at the office. She knew he always arrived early to organize his day before the phones started to ring. Waiting as long as she could stand it, Samantha picked up the phone.

As she dialed Jack's number her mind was racing over the points she wanted to make, organizing them in her mind, then reorganizing. Samantha relaxed as she heard Jack's lazy hello. Jack was the world's most laid-back lawyer. His demeanor and manner of speech had a way of putting you at ease and encouraging you to talk. He was very successful at eliciting information from unsuspecting witnesses and clients. He was easy to trust.

"Jack, it's Samantha." Jack had been a friend of Grant and Samantha's since before they were married. He and Grant had shared a room at law school.

"Samantha, it's good to hear your voice, honey. You doing all right? I know Grant's death must have been hard on you and the children."

"It has been, Jack, and that's one of the reasons I called you. They didn't do an autopsy on Grant."

"Well, honey, that's not surprising, the attending doctor said it was clearly a massive heart attack. I just saw Dr. Sims a couple of days ago. He told me he was amazed that Grant hung on as long as he did. You know he lived for several hours after they got him to the hospital."

"But, Jack, you don't understand," Samantha felt frantic. "I don't think he had a natural heart attack."

"What do you mean?"

"I think that woman caused his heart attack somehow."

Jack felt guilty as he thought, "Rolling around in the hay for a year with Cynthia would probably give anyone a heart attack."

"Do you have something you're basing that belief on, Samantha? That's a pretty serious allegation you're making."

"I don't have any proof, if that's what you mean; Jack; but I know that, if the body were exhumed and autopsied, the evidence would be there. Can you do something to help me?"

"In order to have the body exhumed, we would have to have compelling evidence to show to the District Attorney. We can't get an exhumation order based on suspicion."

Samantha felt like crying. She was a well-informed woman. She knew this would be his answer, but she had to try. Jack felt her frustration in the silence on the telephone.

"Tell you what I'll do, Samantha. I'll talk to a friend of mine down at the station and see if he has any ideas."

"Thanks, Jack, I appreciate it."

Jack held the phone for a few seconds before dropping it back on its cradle. He would mention this business to Bob Martin down at central headquarters. Bob was a good friend. He could look into Cynthia's past quietly to see if there was anything to substantiate Samantha's suspicions or at least to make them seem reasonable. At the moment, Jack felt they were the bitter ruminations of a rejected first wife. Jack had never really understood why Grant left Samantha. Cynthia was a hot little looker, but Samantha was no slouch herself. Grant could have kept his family and had Cynthia on the side. Plenty of men in their group did just that. Jack picked up the phone. Might as well take care of this right now.

"Bob, Jack here. Need a little favor. A little off the record research." Jack quickly related Samantha's suspicions ending with, "I don't really expect you to find anything, but Samantha's an old friend, and I'd like to say I had at least made an effort."

~ ~ ~ ~ ~ ~ ~ ~ ~ ~ ~ ~ ~ ~ ~ ~ ~

Samantha sat in Margaret's driveway staring at the door. She felt very frustrated with Jack's response. She just had to talk with someone about her suspicions. Would Margaret believe her or would she think this was all sour grapes. Grant's mother loved her; she knew that. "If anyone will take me seriously, Margaret will," she thought as she started up the walk. Margaret had seen her drive in and met her at the door.

"Come in, dear, it is so good to see you. Let me make you a cup of coffee."

"Thanks, Margaret, I would like a cup." They sat at the kitchen table talking about the children, the weather, and everything except what Samantha wanted to discuss. Margaret had been patient, but she knew something was troubling Samantha.

Finally she said, "Samantha, something is obviously troubling you. What is it? You know I'll help if I can."

"I don't know if you can help, Mother." Margaret noticed the shift from her given name to the maternal address. Samantha always did this when she felt unsure of herself.

"I'll try," Margaret said. "What's the problem?" Whatever it was, Samantha was having trouble sharing.

"I think Cynthia did something to cause Grant's heart attack. I think she poisoned him or something." Margaret went white as a sheet. Her cup shattered on the floor. She looked as if she might faint.

"Oh, Mother, I'm so sorry, I shouldn't have come to you with this." Samantha rushed around the table to support Margaret. Margaret regained her composure, although, now her cheeks were very flushed indicating to Samantha that her blood pressure had jumped. "You need to lie down, Margaret. Here let me help you."

"No, no, Samantha, I'm okay now. I was just taken off guard. You are still upset over Grant's death, dear. I'm sure Cynthia did nothing to cause it. It was a heart attack, just a heart attack."

Margaret's voice broke and she began crying, uncontrollable, huge, wrenching sobs. Samantha berated herself for being so thoughtless and selfish. She should never have come to Margaret for support on this. Margaret had just lost her only son. She wasn't even over the shock of his death, and now Samantha had burdened her with her own unfounded fears.

"Samantha, you are a callous, thoughtless wretch," she charged herself. Samantha calmed Margaret and stayed until she fell asleep. Even then she felt uneasy leaving her, since Forest was out of town on his annual Big Bass Tournament. This had certainly been a monumental mistake. Dejectedly, she climbed into her car.

Chapter 23

The phone shrilled breaking Cynthia's reverie. Who could be calling so early in the morning? She hadn't even arisen yet.

"Hello," sharply.

"Hello yourself, doll."

"Freddie! Why are you calling here? You know you shouldn't do that."

"We have to talk. I understand you've had an unexpected event." Freddie placed emphasis on unexpected. "My condolences."

"Yes, it was unexpected, but I don't see why we should have to talk."

"I think you do." Freddie's voice sounded very cold.

Cynthia shivered. "When and where?"

"Same place, same time, tomorrow."

"I'll be there." Cynthia didn't like this. She had already paid Freddie half the agreed upon money, but now she didn't need his services. "Perhaps, he is going to return the money," she thought. "No, no way! Freddie would never return easy money. This was certainly easy money," she thought ruefully. "Why couldn't you have waited a little while?" She berated herself. "Always in a hurry, rush, rush, rush. A few more days would have saved you one hundred thousand dollars." She had to admire Freddie though; she knew he had her over a barrel. She could hardly sue for return of the money based on failure to perform the agreed upon service.

~~~~~~~~~~~~~~~~

Cynthia arrived at the river walk early. She wanted this whole mistake behind her. Patrolman Paul Crane noticed the well-dressed woman wandering aimlessly back and forth along the river's edge.

"What is a woman like that doing in this seedy area. Better check it out," he thought. He pulled his cruiser to the side and stepped out. As a matter of routine he informed the dispatcher that he would be out of the cruiser for a few minutes checking out a woman on the riverside. Officer Crane was a rookie, and he drove the dispatcher nuts calling in every time he was out of his vehicle; but, on the other hand, they always knew where he was.

"Nice morning for a walk, isn't it, ma'am?"

Cynthia spun around. "Oh, no, not a policeman," her mind froze momentarily. Officer Crane noticed her anxious look.

"Is there anyway I can be of help?"

"Oh, no," Cynthia gave him a smile. "I'm just out for a walk."

Officer Crane hadn't seen a car. "You walked all the way down here?" He asked incredulously. This woman was obviously from the far side of town. She was wearing an expensive, blue suit with very high heels. Those shoes were definitely not designed for walking, and certainly not for walking several miles.

Cynthia had parked her car several blocks away. Crane suddenly remembered seeing a pale green Jaguar convertible parked four blocks up and one street over. That must be her car, but why would she lie.

"Are you sure you aren't in any difficulty, miss?"

Cynthia smiled sweetly. "No, sir, I'm just having a little walk, enjoying the river."

"Leave," her mind was shrieking. "Please leave."

"Well, all right, if you're sure, you're okay."

"Yes, I'm fine," Cynthia smiled again.

Crane walked back toward his cruiser unconvinced. Women like that didn't frequent the riverside. "Damn, I should have asked her name." He thought about going back, but he knew the chief didn't like to hear anything that sounded like harassment and, if he persisted, it just might be perceived as such. Those uptown folks would call up and complain in a minute. Crane decided that he would just make a couple of extra passes along here this morning.

Freddie watched from the bar. "Damn, stupid bitch," he thought, "she ought to have better sense than to arrive early." A classy dame like her walking, no, pacing, back and forth along the river was sure to attract attention down here. Freddie grinned. On the other hand, Cynthia was a very good actress. She probably had that poor slob eating out of her hand with some cockamamie story of wanting to see the area where her grandparents were born or something. He knew Cynthia well enough to know that she would never admit she grew up down here. He waited until he saw the cruiser move on down the street, then he quickly crossed to the river. Freddie knew the routine and the times that Paul Crane patrolled this area. That's why he scheduled their meeting when he did. Crane would have already made his scheduled drive by.

"Freddie, where have you been," Cynthia's voice shrilled. Her nerves were on edge.

"I'm here right on time, baby," Freddie drawled insolently. "You should know better than to arrive early. I chose eleven o'clock for a reason. Crane has already made his rounds by then." Freddie knew them all by name and on sight. That was just good business. Unfortunately, most of them knew him, too. "Oh, well," Freddie said wryly. "What did you say to the cop?"

"I told him I was out for a walk."

Freddie looked at her with disbelief on his face. "I'm sure he believed that," he snarled. "What a dumb bitch," he thought. Freddie didn't like this. He wanted to finish this quickly before anyone saw them together.

"What do you want, Freddie?" Cynthia blurted.

"What the hell do you think I want? I want the rest of the money."

Cynthia looked at him blankly, "But you didn't do anything. He died of a heart attack."

"Sure, sure he did," Freddie looked at her coldly. "We had a deal. Don't think you can welsh on my fee just because you found a faster way."

"Freddie, he died of a heart attack." Cynthia's heart sank.

She could see the rage building in Freddie. She knew he was dangerous. She had really screwed herself this time. "Okay, Freddie, it will take a few days."

"Not a few days, doll, tomorrow." Freddie looked menacing.

"Okay," Cynthia swallowed hard. She was afraid of the Freddie she saw standing here. Something in him had become hard and mean. What had she been thinking…that some exciting ex-lover from her past could murder her husband and not be cold and mean?

Freddie saw the cruiser and whirled around with his back to the street knowing full well that he would still be recognized. "Damn, see what you've done, Cynthia, you've made him curious. He's having a second look and he's seen us together. If he stops, I'll tell him I saw you over here and thought you might have a problem, so I came over to check."

Officer Crane saw them. "What the hell is a well-dressed, uptown woman doing with Freddie Franklin?" Crane frowned. He thought, "Damn, there is no accounting for taste." Of course, she was slumming. She had probably met Freddie somewhere, and they were having a tawdry little affair. Freddie had a reputation for having a way with the ladies. Crane felt a little disappointed. She seemed like such a sweet lady.

Thirty minutes later, when Officer Crane made his regular pass, they were gone. He swung over to the parallel street. Her car was gone. They'd probably gone somewhere to shack up for a few hours.

~~~~~~~~~~~~~~~~~

Cynthia walked into the First Bank and Trust Company knowing that Bob Tuttle was going to question her closely about making such a big withdrawal in cash, so she had prepared her story.

"Morning, Cynthia," Bob said. "What can I do for you today?"

"I'm getting ready to take a trip, Bob, and I need to draw cash against my credit line."

"How much do you need?" Bob asked prepared to handle the request immediately.

"A hundred thousand," Cynthia said.

Bob gave her a sharp look. "Are you in some kind of trouble, Cynthia? You withdrew a hundred thousand a few days ago."

Cynthia's stomach knotted. "That was for a little shopping spree, Bob. I had to replace my entire wardrobe."

"Why do you need all this cash now? A hundred thousand is a lot of cash."

"I just want to get away for a while, Bob. With Grant gone I just need to be out of the house…maybe for several months."

"Well, you don't want to be carrying that much cash. Let me set up a bank transfer to a bank at your destination."

"You can't do that," Cynthia's mind was searching frantically for a reason. She had it. "Oh, Bob, I'm just going to be traveling without an itinerary, just going wherever my whims take me."

"Well, then we'll make out travelers checks for you."

Cynthia held her temper. Why didn't the old goat just give her the cash? There were times when she enjoyed having men protect her. This was not one of those times. "I'm going directly from here to the American Express office. I really prefer American Express when I'm traveling overseas."

Bob looked somewhat relieved. "I'll have a guard walk you over."

"That won't be necessary. It's just around the corner."

"No, no, I insist, Cynthia. I would never forgive myself if something happened."

"Charlie," he called to one of the guards. "I'd like you to walk Mrs. James over to the American Express office in a few minutes."

Bob completed the paperwork and handed it to Cynthia to sign. He went to the back and returned in a few minutes with a large manila envelope. Cynthia took the envelope, thanked Bob, and left the bank with the guard.

Cynthia stepped into the American Express office. The guard followed her in. "Damn, how am I going to get rid of him," she thought. She smiled at the guard, "Thank you for your help, but I'm safely here now, and I'm sure Mr. Tuttle wants you back as soon as possible."

The guard nodded, smiled, and left. "Well, that was easy enough," she thought. She watched until the guard rounded the corner and then she quickly slipped out the door and walked to her car.

~~~~~~~~~~~~~~~~~

Cynthia appeared at the river walk promptly at eleven o'clock. Suddenly Freddie was beside her. It was unnerving the way he just appeared out of nowhere. Cynthia shoved the envelope at him. He took it as she started to walk away.

DEADLY BREW
She Loved Him to Death

"What's your hurry, baby? Don't want to be seen with me now?" Freddie felt a little bitter. He was good enough to do her dirty work, but it was clear she had no further need of him now. Freddie headed back to the bar feeling a little down and rejected. Life really wasn't fair. He and Cynthia had the same background and ambitions; yet she ended up legitimately wealthy, and he was still down here in the undesirable part of town fighting to be someone.

Chapter 24

Samantha sat staring into the fire. It wasn't really that cold, but she felt chilled to the bone. She faced the upcoming holidays with dread. It would be the first without Grant in her children's lives. She knew she had to be strong to help them get past the sorrow. She wished she could include Peter in the festivities, but Trey and Sadie did not know he existed. She had been very careful not to mention him. She feared that her children were not ready for someone special in her life. It just wasn't the time to make them aware that she was moving ahead, trying to make a new life for herself. His presence would be such a pillar of strength for her, but she couldn't indulge herself now. Peter would be disappointed that they could not be together, but he would understand. He knew as she did what pain and trauma resulted from a loss of a parent.

Samantha wanted to keep the children busy with planned activities. She would suggest that they go to the Christmas tree farm to select and cut the perfect tree. Then, they could plan a decorating party and invite Grandmother and Grandfather James. Margaret would love to prepare the treats for the kids. An open house for all the children's friends would be a special surprise for them. Her mind raced on and on trying to fill as much time as possible. She didn't want to chance too much idle time. She would insist that they needed to start new traditions. Sadie had mentioned going to visit the children's ward at all the local hospitals. Together they could make a small gift for each of the children. Trey could be quite a clown when called upon. "Nothing cheers a person more than bringing happiness to someone else," she thought. It would be fun also to go caroling door to door. Of course, Sadie and Trey would make a big production of asking her to "please lip sync." Oh, well, she would let them have their fun. She would carry the flashlight.

They had always attended midnight mass on Christmas Eve. Samantha decided that she would prepare a special buffet and make it a more festive occasion. She could pick up one of those Christmas puzzles. It might be fun to tell Sadie and Trey they couldn't open their gifts until it was finished. Grandmother James had already invited them to Christmas dinner at her house. Samantha would suggest that they take along several games to play. Scrabble was always fun, but it was hard to beat Forest. Sadie and Trey were dynamite at Trivial Pursuit. She and Margaret would have to come up with something they could win. On second thought, maybe this was a good year to buy everyone a toy…a remote control car so they could have races. Yes, that would be good. They all needed a little lighthearted laughter. Samantha felt sure they could make this a merry Christmas after all.

Chapter 25

Samantha looked up as Trey entered the room. There was something about him that made her become instantly alert. He had a perplexed expression and was staring at a paper in his hand. "Trey, is something wrong?" she asked quietly.

"I'm not sure. Cynthia met me on campus today and asked me to sign this document about Dad's estate. I told her I wanted to talk with you first. She offered me five hundred dollars so we could get this resolved quickly. She said she had mailed Sadie the same thing. Why would she do that, Mom? We know she was Dad's beneficiary for his insurance. I still don't understand why he didn't name Sadie and me on that policy. And it is unbelievable that he didn't have a will. He was an estate attorney, for pete's sake."

Samantha shook her head and reached for the document in Trey's hand. Maybe he had misunderstood Cynthia. Samantha's brow creased as she read the paper. "I think we should call Jack. He's our friend so we can trust him to give us an honest opinion."

~~~~~~~~~~~~~~~~~

Jack raised his eyes from the document frowning. "It appears she is trying to pay the children to sign away any further interest in their father's estate. I thought there was nothing left after debts were settled. Something doesn't ring right here. Samantha, what kind of assets did Grant have after your divorce?"

Samantha sighed, "Not a lot, you know Grant made some bad investments shortly before our divorce. He had the Brookston stock, but I think he sold all of that to Sam to pay for Sadie's college. He had the Mercedes, jewelry, tools, golf clubs, the country club membership, and the country house."

Jack straightened. "How was the country house titled?"

Samantha shook her head, "I really don't know. I signed a quitclaim deed. What difference would that make?"

Jack stood up and started pacing. "Maybe none, but if it was held tenants in common as compared to joint tenancy with right of survivorship, Cynthia would only be entitled to her half plus a spousal share or one-third of the value of the remaining half, which would mean that the children would be entitled to the other two-thirds. Since he had planned to sell it, she may have let that slip past her."

Samantha stared out the window. "She has been very uncooperative with the children. She has held tight to his personal possessions. Trey wanted his dad's golf equipment and guns, but she has refused to let go of anything. She was down right rude to Sadie when she mentioned her desire for some keepsakes.

I've been suppressing my anger for the children's sake. I didn't want anyone yelling sour grapes at my attitude, but, dammit, Jack, that woman is a she-devil. Don't let her cheat my children. She's already deprived them of their father at a crucial time in their lives. I want you to find out what she's up to and stop it. She has stolen enough from all of us. No more! Do you understand me, Jack? No more!"

Jack walked to Samantha and put his arm around her shoulders. "I'll get right on it, Samantha. I won't let her hurt you or the children anymore. You have my promise; if there is something amiss, I'll find out and put a halt to it. Your children will get the things they deserve from Grant's estate. Tell the kids not to sign anything, and I'll be in touch."

Jack led her to the door and watched as she walked down the hall. Grant had been a fool to leave her, but lust does strange things to a man. Grant had been an outstanding attorney. Jack couldn't believe he had not provided for his children in the event of his death. Hell, he of all people should have had a will. After all, Trey had still been living with his dad. It just didn't make sense. He intended to get to the bottom of this pronto. What was Cynthia's problem? She was a wealthy woman. She had inherited all of Roderick's estate. Why would she try to cheat those kids? Was she truly as wicked and greedy as Samantha implied?

Jack's investigation was very revealing. Cynthia was smart. She knew the children were entitled to two-thirds of Grant's share of the proceeds from the country house. She had hoped to pay them five hundred dollars to sign away their interest, thus legally cheating them. Jack was furious. They would have their day in court. The kids would get their just settlement plus the personal possessions they wanted. Jack hated greedy people. He had always thought Cynthia a very sexy little number, but he was liking her less and less as he got to see the real Cynthia. Grant must have been blind. However, the last several times he talked with Grant before his death, Grant had seemed withdrawn. He'd even made comments about missing his family. Jack had taken that to mean his children, but now he wondered if Grant was having serious regrets about Samantha, too. The poor bastard lost it all for a piece of ass. If Grant knew what Cynthia was trying to do, he'd turn over in his grave. His kids had always been very important to him. He was very proud of them. What a shame his untimely death had been. He might have put things back together if he had lived.

~~~~~~~~~~~~~~~~

Cynthia was shocked when she received the letter from her attorney advising her that the renunciation sent to Sadie and Trey had been returned unsigned by their attorney, Jack Reed.

"Damn, the little bastards are smarter than I thought," Cynthia said angrily. Jack had reminded her attorney that renunciations were to be executed in the first nine months of probate. It was too late now.

Jack had also noted that it was interesting that the renunciation arrived one year and one day after Trey's twenty-first birthday, noting that his majority would have prevented a contest had he been eager for a quick five hundred dollars.

Cynthia was seething by the time she finished reading Jack's scathing letter to her attorney. "That low life shyster, some friend he is!" She picked up the phone and dialed.

"Mr. Shipman's office, may I help you?"

"Jackie, this is Cynthia James, may I speak to Jay?"

Cynthia tapped her sculpted nails on her marble desktop. She was scheming again. There had to be another way to prevent Grant's brats from taking her country home away from her. It had nothing to do with attachment to the house. It was a turn of the century monstrosity that was cold and drafty in the winter and hot in the summer. The cost to update was more than she wanted to invest in something she had no intention of ever stepping foot into again in this lifetime. True, it was in a lovely setting and would probably sell quickly to some urbanite that needed to get away from the city. "Give me sidewalks and neon lights, to hell with mosquitoes, chiggers, and nature. Grant was so ordinary when it came to things like the country house."

"Cynthia, I presume you've received my letter."

"Yes, which way do we proceed now? Jay, please don't think I'm selfish and greedy, but I invested a great deal of my money in renovating that house. I love it, but without Grant, I just can't go back," Cynthia sighed dramatically. "It's too painful. However, I can't just let it sit there. Grant would have wanted me to protect my investment, and you understand, if I have to split the proceeds for the sale with his children, I'll be losing my own money. It would be different if they were my children, also. Grant provided for his children in other ways before his death. He made sure everything for his children flowed directly to them and bypassed probate."

"Cynthia, this property was Grant's after his divorce. When he added your name to the deed it did not specify that it was 'joint tenants with right of survivorship.' It only said husband and wife. As I explained before, statutes require the magic words of 'joint tenants with right of survivorship' or it is presumed 'tenancy in common.' The way it is written you'd only be entitled to your one-half and a child's share of the other half."

"Can't we argue the increased value during the marriage, my assistance in bringing the mortgage payments up to date, and the remodeling?"

"Sure, but you will need to provide me with canceled checks, receipts, and appraisals on the house at the time Grant was divorced and now. The court isn't going to automatically accept our argument."

"O...K..., but what if all those checks and receipts were destroyed when our warehouse flooded the last winter Grant was alive?"

"Are you telling me you do not have any evidence?" Jay didn't like the sound of that.

"Yes and no! No, because the plumbing froze and burst over the holidays that year and flooded the warehouse where they were stored. All my records were in cardboard file boxes, a total loss by the time we returned from Vail after New Year. I'm sure the contractor would be willing to testify to my investment, and then the mortgage company can show Grant was on the verge of foreclosure when we married. Some of these records may be hard to find. Grant wasn't the most organized person in the world."

"This might be easy if the kids and their mother aren't in a position or of a mind to fight it out in a long court battle, then maybe not!" Jay speculated.

Cynthia hung up the phone and immediately started her destruction list.

1. Call Carla at the bank. She owes me big time – microfiche.
2. Call Charlie, I bailed him out on his last two construction projects.
3. Call Bill, he did the property evaluation for Grant when he first purchased the country house – get a copy.
4. Call Rick to get a new appraisal – fax a copy of Bill's original appraisal.
5. Research who can see that all copies of the appraisal done for the property settlement between Grant and Samantha are lost.

Jay filed the Application for the Final Decree of Distribution feeling confident with the evidence and witnesses Cynthia produced. There shouldn't be any fall out from the other heirs, but he was ready to defend Cynthia's interest in the country house, if opposed.

Cynthia felt very smug as she read the legal document in front of her. Jay was so good! She almost believed it. It was all coming together. When Jack received his copy, there is no way they would object. Jay had documented her right to one hundred percent of this property, cited strings of cases to support his position with extensive exhibits as proof.

~~~~~~~~~~~~~~~~

Jack was on a mission. Grant James had been his friend, and he knew Grant never would have left his children with nothing but memories and a few worthless mementoes. He couldn't believe what he was reading. Shipman had certainly pulled out all the stops. What a bunch of trumped up legal BS. He snatched the hand recorder and began firing his objections to the application.

Jack had groaned when he learned the hearing would be before District Judge Parker Henry. Parker had hated Grant, but there was nothing to be done about it. Parker had not recused himself. The hearing before Judge Henry was heated. Jay objected to the arguments and exhibits produced by Jack. He challenged. Authentication lacking, best evidence rule violated, cumulative, foundation lacking, immaterial and irrelevant were his favorites.

Cynthia was getting nervous. This wasn't going as she had planned. How did Jack track down all those real estate transactions in which she had been involved? "She is sophisticated in real estate," Jack had alleged. Hell, yes, she was, but Jay had to mitigate that damage on redirect.

"Where is that damn Charlie! Jay told him to be here at nine forty-five a.m. sharp," Cynthia raged. "This is not going well! Our argument that the deed was titled incorrectly through a scrivener's error sounds very weak considering Grant's associate prepared it for us."

Jay appeared calm and composed, but Cynthia felt warm and uncomfortable. She dabbed her forehead and dreaded taking the stand.

Trey and Sadie kept staring at her. She expected hostility from Sadie, but she always thought Trey was rather enamored of her. "I'm sure sweet little Samantha's been poisoning his mind since Grant's death." Groaning inwardly she wondered, "Will this hearing ever end?"

"I call Cynthia James to the stand."

Cynthia thought the ordeal was almost over until the cross-examination by Jack. He really knew more about her relationship with Grant than she expected. Was it supposition or did he have evidence unknown to Jay and her? How much did Grant discuss their private life and finances? After one particularly pregnant silence, Jay objected hoping to break Jack's momentum but was overruled for a lack of valid grounds. Cynthia was reaching for the politically correct answers while inside she wanted to get downright vicious. Jack had done his homework. In fact, it was obvious he had been working overtime to collect this much information since the application was filed. Surprisingly, Judge Henry was ruling in Jack's favor. "Maybe, he has finally forgiven Grant's transgression with Penelope," Jack thought.

The judge took it under advisement, but Cynthia left the courtroom knowing in her heart the battle lines had been drawn. A few days later, her suspicions were validated. Motion to deny her administration fee for undue delay was filed along with a motion for sanctions for commingling estate funds with her personal accounts. She felt the tide begin to turn against her.

"How in the hell did they discover these things?" She would love to argue ignorance but she had been Roderick's personal representative on an estate much larger than this paltry sum. She was beginning to look like the "wicked stepmother" that she was. She really didn't care what Samantha and her brats thought of her, but word was getting around and more spectators were appearing each time a hearing was set.

Jay was willing to fight it to the end but advised Cynthia that a settlement might be in her best interest. Speaking of interest, he was sure that he could limit the rate to the "contract rate" on any judgment or settlement. There was a long-standing case to that effect. Cynthia was to think about it before the next hearing. Cynthia didn't like the odds. She was a seasoned gambler, and she could see that if Jack delved much deeper she would feel too exposed. She hated to give up even one red cent, but knew when to fold…it was in her best interest to settle.

Chapter 26

Freddie saw the flashing blue light in his rearview mirror. "Dammit." He only had another six months on that five-year suspended sentence for assault and battery, and here he was drunker than a bootlegger at his pappy's funeral. As the officer approached the car and asked him to step out and present his driver's license, a sick feeling washed over him. If this guy found any reason to search his car, the concealed weapon under his seat would be the knot in the noose that would hang him. He wasn't supposed to possess a firearm after conviction of a felony. His fate would be sealed by these charges.

"Good evening, officer, what seems to be the problem?"

Officer Hilliard was tired. It was one hour until shift change, and he wasn't in the mood for bullshit. "Problem? You tell me! You just cruised through a red light, failed to signal when you turned, and curbed your vehicle. That's what you might call a problem."

"Ah, come on, officer, I was just headed home after a night of hard work. Tired, that's my problem, I'm bone tired."

As the officer waited for Freddie's license, he retorted, "I'd say bottle tired, in fact, bottom of the bottle tired. Now, where is your license?"

Freddie reluctantly produced his license. Now the guy would run a check, and the rest would be history. Freddie knew from past experience that convicted felons had no rights even after they served their time.

"Can't you give me a break, officer, it's late and I have an early day tomorrow."

The officer looked at him like he was less than an ant. Freddie's blood boiled but he knew he had to keep his cool. He was in deep stuff here and he knew it.

"Okay, buddy, let's see how tired you are. Step out of the car. Close your eyes." Freddie complied. "Now put your arms straight out to each side. Touch your nose with your right pointer finger, now left. Pretty shaky. See that white line along the shoulder, walk it for me." Freddie collected all his faculties and maneuvered the line acceptably much to the chagrin of Officer Hilliard.

"Mister, you claim you're just tired, but I smell alcohol on you. You're a pathetic driver. Your vehicle doesn't have a valid inspection sticker. Let me see your registration." Freddie started to climb into the car. "Just a minute," Officer Hilliard said. "Where is it?"

"In the glove compartment," Freddie said.

"Come around to the other side." Hilliard unsnapped his gun. "Open your door and reach in with your left hand. Keep your right hand over your head." Freddie was in a panic. He knew the registration wasn't in the glove box. He had purchased his Jaguar through the "grey market" and had never received a valid title. The tag on his car belonged to another vehicle. "I can't find it. I must have lost it," he attempted.

"All right, step out and put your hands on the car. Spread your legs." Officer Hilliard radioed for backup, then he began to pat Freddie down for weapons. He figured they would find an open container and maybe even drugs in Freddie's car; but he didn't want to handle a search without assistance, especially at this hour of the night.

Hilliard knew his backup should be here shortly. Freddie Franklin was definitely intoxicated and had no registration and probably a carload of open containers. He could see the flashing lights of the approaching cruiser, so he advised Freddie to move. Officer Lester approached with caution but on full adrenaline alert in case things fell apart.

"Who have we got here?" Lester inquired.

"Frederick Joseph Franklin, who can't lie worth a damn."

"Where's his license and we'll see just exactly who Mr. Franklin is and if he has ever been a guest of the Cantrell County Hilton." Usually guys like Freddie had spent more than one night at the county's expense.

The radio crackled. The dispatcher recited the lengthy resume of Freddie's criminal qualifications, and previous affiliation with the "Big White House." Lester's brow furrowed as he heard that the tag didn't belong to this particular car. Hilliard was approaching Lester's car with Franklin in cuffs. The recitation of the Miranda Rights echoed in the still night air. Lester opened the back cage and shoved the very drunk Freddie into the dark cavity.

As they returned to Franklin's vehicle, Lester said, "The tag is not a match."

"What is the match?"

"Can't recall exactly but it damn sure wasn't a Jaguar registered to Franklin."

As they began the search, Hilliard ran his hand under the seat and felt the cold metal...a pipe? No, no, son-of-a-bitch, a big hog! A nine-millimeter with a silencer! What in the hell was this idiot doing with a gun this size plus a silencer. Lester was searching the trunk when he heard Hilliard exclaim. He found his fellow officer with a case of the jitters and a cannon in his hand. No explanation was necessary. The "what ifs" were endless. It was a good thing Hilliard waited for backup before searching and cuffing Franklin. It could have turned lethal from the get go. If Hilliard believed in guardian angels, his was definitely working the night shift.

"This guy has served time for killing a couple of guys. Must have been one hell of a plea or some mitigating circumstances. I guess we'll know more after he's booked and the DA gets a look."

~~~~~~~~~~~~~~~~

DEADLY BREW
She Loved Him to Death

It was about nine a.m. when Sgt. Martin finished his morning ritual, two cups of stiff black coffee, a chocolate glazed donut, and the USA Today paper. He drifted through the office catching up on the previous night's developments. He had noticed that one Freddie Joseph Franklin was booked in the early hours. Why was that name so familiar?

Martin meandered down the hallway and noticed that the door to the interrogation room was closed. "Wonder which low life we have in there at this early hour?" He opened the door to the observation area and had a seat. The face was remotely familiar. He listened for a couple minutes and decided this could be interesting.

"Freddie, you keep saying you have something worth making a deal, but you're giving us nothing. You either talk and do it fast or we're out of here, and your ass can rot in the state lockup for the next forty years."

Freddie ran his hand through his hair. He was tired, hot, and nervous as a whore in church on Sunday. He damn sure didn't want to go back to the joint. He cringed at the thought and felt a cold sweat starting to bead. He could act like a tough son-of-a-bitch out here, but this kind of bullshit didn't cut it in the big house.

"Ok, ok, I can deliver you a killer…premeditated." This got Lt. Gardner's attention as he stopped pacing and moved to the chair across from Freddie. In the observation room Sgt. Martin sat up straight, more alert now.

"Yeah, right, let me guess…the guy is behind the walls, or he has skipped but you know his name."

"No, no, it's not a man!"

Gardner straightened his shoulders. "Are we talking juvenile, or female, or maybe both?"

"Woman, dammit, one good looking broad. I mean rich, sexy, and prominent!"

Sgt. Martin had been ready to step out of the observation room when he stopped mid-stride. "Rich…good looking…prominent…" It was almost like watching a movie in slow motion as Martin's mind's eye got an instant "still shot" of a drop dead good-looking, leggy blonde in a sexy, short skirt. "Hell, what was it Jack mentioned to me awhile back? It was a favor to a friend…someone had died unexpectedly…someone was suspicious of the second wife…what was the name…Cynthia something."

At that moment Freddie said, "Cynthia James, formerly know as Barker."

Lt. Gardner exhaled, "Cynthia James, as in Grant James' widow? Give me a break, you pea-brained cockroach."

Martin eased back in the chair giving full attention to Freddie.

"Do we have a deal or not?"

"Freddie, you've been down this road before; you know I can't make any promises. But considering the vast difference between your charges and those of a premeditated murder, I'd say with evidence to support a conviction, Mad Dog will go the length in settling your matter without your serving time."

Martin joined Gardner as Freddie began to talk. "It all started when she approached me in a little place on the river…"

By the time Freddie had finished his story, Sgt. Martin was convinced that this was not a cock and bull story. He needed to talk with Jack again. This was big and they sure as hell better handle it by the book.

Chapter 27

Samantha was tense when she awakened at three o'clock a.m. She had been asleep only two hours. She had finally won. Grant's body was going to be exhumed.

Grant had been dead eleven months, and his death had haunted her ever since the moment she called Mildred that dreadful night. She didn't believe a perfectly healthy man could just drop dead of a heart attack. Grant had yearly physicals. He was in excellent health and worked hard to keep himself that way. He was fit and lean. He played golf, racquetball, and did fifty sit-ups daily. His thorough physicals had never indicated even the slightest abnormality in his heart. Yes, his doctors had told him to slow down and smell the roses, but that was supposed to be a precaution not a necessity.

Samantha remembered the white roses at the church. Cynthia didn't know Grant at all, or she would have known he hated white roses. Samantha recalled that it had something to do with his grandfather's funeral when he was a child. Samantha listened to the sounds of the night marking the seconds until dawn. This was going to be a long arduous day. Samantha looked forward to the day with dread. She didn't want to attend the exhumation, but she felt she had to go. Samantha felt like a character in someone else's dark nursery rhyme.

"Patty cake, patty cake, coroner's man. Dig up a grave as fast as you can."

Grant had played a tragic game of patty cake with Cynthia. She baked him a pretty cake with lots of blonde icing to make it sweet. She marked him with a "D" for dead, and put him in a big pan with a lid, and served him up with white roses.

"Get a grip, Samantha," she told herself, "you're about over the edge."

Tomorrow, no, today, in fact within a few hours, Grant would be removed from his final resting place. Samantha was speaking aloud now.

"Oh, Grant, it still hurts so much. I was healing, laughing again, enjoying being a real woman again. Peter has been good for me. I have a life now, Grant. It's been like an initiation into a big new club, but I can't abandon you. I was making new friends, attracting the admiring glances of the male gender and feeling very much alive until you died. I know she killed you, Grant, I know that."

"Someone had to remain strong and seek some answers. Grant, you were wrong in what you did to me and the children. I'm trying to forgive you for the hurt you caused us. It wouldn't have been so bad if it had only been me, but you hurt the children. Nothing was ever the same after the divorce. I was angry with you, Grant, but I never wanted you dead. In the beginning, I wanted to strangle that blonde bitch with my bare hands. Maybe I should have, then you would be alive now."

Samantha realized she was speaking aloud to a dead man. She looked at the clock…six o'clock a.m. Samantha thought, "Will your spirit be freed by this exhumation? Will you rest in peace once we have some answers? Oh, Grant, this could have been so different."

Samantha wept quietly into her pillow. Exhausted, she dozed for two hours. She woke with a start as her alarm erupted. Groggily, she reached to shut it off. She pulled herself out of bed and staggered to the kitchen. The coffeemaker had brewed a pot of solid gold salvation. One cup…she might survive; two cups should fortify her enough to get dressed and add a touch of blush and lipstick. She didn't have to go to the cemetery but she felt a need to be there.

"You must be off your rocker," Samantha admonished herself as she drove to the cemetery. This exhumation could be more traumatic than the funeral. The minister had said the words "…laid to rest…eternal peace…"

"Have I done the right thing," she agonized. "Grant deserves justice," she kept repeating. "Grant, I promise I'll be strong. I'll see this thing through. We all need some closure."

As Samantha drove through the gate of the Garden of Tranquility cemetery, she had to stop and take a deep breath. She was having an anxiety attack. She felt her chest tighten, her breathing came quickly, and she felt momentarily dizzy.

"Breathe deeply…in…hold…exhale slowly…in…hold…exhale slowly. There that's better. God, please grant me the strength and serenity to get through this day."

The van from the coroner's office was parked on the grass near Grant's grave. The backhoe looked strangely out of place, as the workmen with shovels stood at uneasy attention like soldiers ready for battle. Sam Warfield and an official looking man stood watching. Samantha stopped on the road adjacent to the site. A glance in her rearview mirror told her that Detective Sgt. Martin was on her schedule. He parked his department issue, plain, navy blue sedan within inches of her bumper. Samantha chuckled thinking this was a sign that this man liked to live dangerously and walk on the edge. Sobering, she told herself, "Just the type necessary to pursue and snare the beautiful, blonde Cynthia 'Black Widow' James."

"Good morning, Sgt. Martin, I see my timing is excellent."

"Mrs. James…"

"Please call me Samantha, technically I'm no longer Mrs. James."

"Are you sure that you want to be here? You know, it's not necessary."

"Sgt. Martin, I appreciate your concern, but I feel it is my duty. After all, I was married to Grant for twenty-three years. We have two children who love their father very much."

Sgt. Martin mentally noted that she was speaking in the present tense. It was obvious that this woman had not accepted her husband's death...ex-husband, that is. Sam Warfield nodded his head at the workmen and the backhoe roared to life. The backhoe moved the few feet of dirt in short order. As they neared the vault the shovel made a sharp grating sound. The backhoe backed up and the men with the shovels took over. They began the tedious chore of clearing the vault cover. A yell from a man in the hole soon announced, "We're there." The men crawled out of the hole, and Sam stepped forward to direct the activities. His eyes met Samantha's. With a nod to her, he quietly issued instructions. Samantha's attention was drawn toward the road. Cynthia was stepping out of a car with two men whom Samantha recognized as lawyers. "You'll need them," Samantha thought bitterly.

Cynthia was furious with the DA, the coroner, and with Samantha. "This is all that spiteful bitch's doings," thought an enraged Cynthia. "She wasn't woman enough to hold her man and now she is out to get me. I'll have the last laugh; they won't find anything in an autopsy. Good heavens, Grant has been embalmed and in the ground for almost a year now." Cynthia was a little nervous, however. She had heard that Freddie had been picked up on a DUI and a concealed weapons charge. It was ironic that she had been returning from a meeting with Freddie at the time Grant had his heart attack. It would have saved her money if he had died a half-hour earlier, but there had been no delaying Freddie. Cynthia remembered how Freddie had laughed when she told him Grant had died of a heart attack and she didn't owe him any more money. It was an ugly laugh from a dangerous man who demanded the remainder of the money, since, as he put it, the end result was the same...a dead husband. Cynthia was afraid to say no, so she had obtained the money and given it to him. But now Freddie had been arrested and Cynthia felt uneasy. What if someone discovered the connection? Freddie wouldn't talk. He couldn't, he took the money and agreed to do the job even though it became unnecessary. That made him too involved to talk.

The assistant chief medical examiner, George W. Richards, rode back to the county morgue with Sam Warfield. Sam was curious as to how the DA was able to get the cooperation of the office of the Chief Medical Examiner to exhume Grant James' body.

"George, you don't have to answer if I'm out of line asking but with all due respect, I know that we have to consider public interest and assist in determining cause or manner of death when there are suspicious or unanswered questions, but it seems we're reaching on this one. How did Samantha James make this happen?"

"Sam, you know as well as I do that we're not bound by statute to honor a private citizens request alone."

"So you're saying there is more? What, for heavens sake! The attending physician said heart attack. Happens all the time. What's suspicious or unusual about that? If I remember Title 633938 correctly, the only two criteria that we could possibly try to stretch would be death under suspicious, unusual, or unnatural circumstances, which I've already ruled out, and death of persons after unexplained coma, and that seems to go with heart attacks, strokes, etc...So why?"

George didn't comment but gave Sam a raised eyebrow. Sam knew when he'd gone too far. "I guess I'm just overreacting, but please tell me, did I miss something obvious that required an autopsy immediately after death?"

"Sam, you know that the attending physician has the responsibility to notify the County Medical Examiner or the DA when further investigation is needed."

"Yes, but Grant was healthy as far as everyone knew until his heart attack. Since I didn't need an autopsy authorization, and he was a friend, I should have taken some specimens of blood, fluids or waste. I should have taken it upon myself. It was my duty to ascertain if the certification of death was correct. I should have questioned his death."

~ ~ ~ ~ ~ ~ ~ ~ ~ ~ ~ ~ ~ ~ ~ ~

The doorbell rang. Cynthia was expecting Walter Meade. She had been dating him for about nine months now. He was somewhat younger than Grant, but quite wealthy. She definitely wasn't having any more financially insolvent men in her life. She was still fuming, regarding the outcome of the probate. "Who would have thought that prissy Samantha would have duplicate copies of everything pertaining to the country house? Curse that damn contractor for not showing up. She'd paid him well. She'd heard he liked the bottle. Probably got cold feet. Spineless jerk! She'd get even with him somehow. She had wanted to wipe that smirk off Samantha's face when the judge ruled that Sadie and Trey were entitled to their share. If "miss prim and proper" had stayed out of it, Cynthia was sure the brats could have been bought. Damn her rotten luck. After all the favors she called in, she felt doubly cheated.

Cynthia transformed her face into a radiant, smiling visage, hesitated a moment then opened the door with a flourish. "I've been waiting..." Cynthia broke off. It was not Walter Meade facing her but Detective Sgt. Martin of the homicide department. Cynthia's throat tightened. "Sgt. Martin, what are you doing here?"

Sgt. Martin had an uniformed officer with him, she noted. He cleared his throat. "Cynthia James, you are under arrest for the murder of Grant James."

Cynthia blanched, "What are you talking about?" She stammered. "Grant had a heart attack. I want to call my lawyer."

"There will be a plenty of time for that at the station." He turned to the uniformed officer. "Cuff her and read her rights."

Sgt. Martin stepped aside as the officer cuffed Cynthia. He took a small card from his pocket and droned, "You have the right to remain silent. If you give up the right to remain silent, anything you say can and will be used against you in a court of law. You have the right to speak with an attorney and to have the attorney present during questioning. If you so desire and cannot afford one, an attorney will be appointed for you without charge before the questioning begins. Do you understand your rights as I have read them to you?"

"Do you understand?" he repeated.

Cynthia nodded numbly. She was crying now. This couldn't be happening. Grant had a heart attack. Cynthia looked imploringly at Sgt. Martin. "I didn't kill Grant," she sobbed. "He had a heart attack."

The ride to the station took an eternity. The handcuffs were uncomfortable. Cynthia recalled the shocked look on Mildred's face. Not a word had been exchanged. Cynthia realized she had forgotten about Walter. Whatever would Mildred tell him? Cynthia was placed in a holding room until her attorney arrived. She was then taken through the normal booking procedures. Her attorney assured her he would have her out quickly.

Since this was a capital crime she would have to remain incarcerated until a hearing could be arranged. He assured her that she would have to be arraigned within seventy-two hours. A hearing would have to occur within ten days. "Ten days," Cynthia exclaimed and began to cry softly. "I didn't kill Grant, I don't understand why I'm here." Deep inside her there was an insidious thought growing. "Freddie. Did Freddie have anything to do with this?"

Chapter 28

Samantha, Sadie, and Trey sat with Margaret and Forest, on the left side of the courtroom directly behind the prosecutor's table, which was beside the jury box. The prosecutor wanted to make sure the jury saw the family, the people who were hurt the most by this murder. Margaret seemed excessively distressed and had not wanted to come today, but Samantha insisted that they must stand united. Samantha understood why Margaret hated to relive all the unhappiness. However, considering that Cynthia killed her only son, one would think she would want to be here to see justice done. The prosecutor, Roberta Marshall, was a young woman in her early thirties with dark hair and intense brown eyes. Rumor had it that some defense attorneys referred to her as 'Mad Dog.' Friends from law school called her 'Rocky.' She had the reputation of being as tenacious and tough as Rocky and as good looking as Sly.

According to Sgt. Martin, the prosecution had a pretty solid case against Cynthia. The coroner's results, the hitman's testimony, the eyewitness testimony linking Cynthia with the hitman, plus the circumstantial evidence were very incriminating.

Today would be jury selection. Twelve 'good men and true' from this county would be selected based on questioning by the prosecution and defense. Jack had told Samantha that jurors would be questioned about education, relationship to anyone involved in the case, and their prejudices or personal situations.

Bradford P. Harmon, Cynthia's lead lawyer, used his preemptors early in the voir dire. He reached for threads to challenge for cause on a few prospective jurors but was overruled on most.

Roberta was amused to see her ex-lover among the prospective jurors. She knew that Harmon had done his homework when he immediately asked, "Do you know anyone in the District Attorney's office?"

Response with a smile, "Yes."

"Do you know this person other than as a public servant?"

Pause. "Yes."

"How well do you know this person?"

Smile. "Very well."

Harmon looked at Roberta and then said, "I'd like to excuse this juror, Your Honor."

Roberta used her preemptors more cautiously, but didn't find the need to challenge as many prospective jurors as Mr. Harmon. This appeared to be a custom ordered panel for a prosecutor. There was a good cross-section of the county. She was able to qualify three middle class women, who had been divorced and reared children with little or no assistance. The blue-collar males were always good when confronted with a rich, self-sufficient female. Then, there was the black grandmother with a lifetime experience of hardship. The ringer would be Sarah, the middle class Manager of Division Orders for a major oil company. She was obviously very detail oriented, attentive, and analytical. Roberta would bet her week's wages that Sarah would be the foreman.

After two days of voir dire, the jury was sworn in and the judge recited their duties as related to the trial. He enumerated the restrictions and responsibilities during sequestration of the panel. This was a highly publicized case and to prevent any outside influence from tainting the jury, special arrangements were necessary.

The trial began on the third day with Roberta Marshall giving a strong, captivating opening statement. As she detailed what she planned to prove in the case, her intense eye contact with the jury kept them at rapt attention. She was good with juries. Being of an expressive heritage she talked with her hands…not distracting gyrations, but welcoming, open, and "trust me" types of movement.

Although, Roberta had tried many capital jury cases, this was different. She was up against the best. Bradford P. Harmon had an extraordinary track record. She could learn from a true master, the Guru, the man with the jeweled turban. She should be intimidated but she wasn't. She was confident in her ability and the prosecution's case.

She looked every bit the part in her black suit and low healed, black pumps. She was a practical, no nonsense, professional. The starkness of her attire did not detract from the compelling personality that captivated the jury during her opening and closing statements.

Bradford P. Harmon's appearance did not belie the consummate high dollar defense attorney he was. His custom tailored, navy, pinstriped suit, his monogrammed shirt with diamond stud cuff links, Presidential Rolex watch and expensive Italian loafers shouted his success. His reputation was legendary. His record in criminal defense hadn't been matched in recent history.

His charm and wit were mesmerizing. His steel gray eyes and salt and pepper hair stylishly brushed back to slightly touch his collar instilled a feeling of confidence and trust; however, those who knew B.P. Harmon were also acquainted with his skills as a trained predator in the courtroom. He knew how to seek out and hypnotize his prey. Like a cobra, he lured those who watched into the rhythm of his trap. It was easy to forget he was a slick operator, a champion of the rich and famous who chose to disregard the mores of society, the laws of the land and God!

As the trial progressed, Roberta found herself being sucked into his circle. He was more than a worthy opponent. He exuded total confidence. The jurors were almost bowing in reverence to his very presence. She realized that the only way to break the spell would be to present an objection, which she knew, would cause a momentary fracture to their rapt attention. Knowing she would be overruled, she stood, "Objection. Wealth of party mentioned and personal belief in merits expressed."

"Overruled."

Roberta hated to make frivolous objections, which tended to aggravate the judge, but the necessity outweighed the scolding look from Judge Summerfield.

Recapturing her composure, she proceeded with the State's first witness, the Chief Medical Examiner.

"Mr. Carlson, will you state your credentials." Roberta stood patiently while the CME droned out a long list of credentials.

"Your Honor, the State requests that Mr. Carlson be recognized as an expert witness."

After going through all the formalities, Roberta began to ask specific questions designed to elicit cause of death.

"Digitalis poisoning leading to a fatal heart attack."

"Where was it found?"

"In the skeletal muscles."

"How long does it take for digitalis to cause death?"

"The time varies depending on the compound it is in and the quantity of the dose."

"Can you give us a range of time?"

"From immediate up to six to eight hours later. In this case it was immediate."

There was a long series of presentations by the CME explaining how he came to that conclusion. Roberta was surprised when on cross-examination Harmon only asked a few perfunctory questions.

"State calls Patti Burleson."

Patti, looking distressed and pale, came forward. She didn't want to be involved. She was so sorry she had mentioned to Mildred that she had noticed the only thing of Roderick Barker's left in the house was his medicine.

"Do you swear to tell the truth..." Patti barely heard the bailiff swear her in.

"State your name and occupation, please."

"My name is Patti Burleson and I am a wedding coordinator."

"Ms. Burleson, in 1993 did you plan and organize a wedding for Cynthia Barker and Grant James?"

"I did."

"Do you see Cynthia Barker James in this room?"

"I do."

"Can you point to Mrs. James? Let the record show that Ms. Burleson has pointed to the defendant, Cynthia Barker James. When and where did that wedding take place?"

"The wedding took place in the United Methodist Church on October 18, 1993."

"Did you ever have an occasion to be in Mrs. James' home?"

"I did."

"How often were you in Mrs. James' home?"

"On several occasions while we were planning the wedding."

"And where did these meetings take place?"

"What do you mean?" Patti looked confused.

"In what part of the house did you and Mrs. James have your meetings?"

"Objection, irrelevant."

"Where are you going with this Ms. Marshall?"

"If you will bear with me, Your Honor, I will show it goes to the issue in question."

"Overruled. Answer the question Ms. Burleson."

"Oh, mostly in her parlor."

"Did you ever have occasion to be in any other part of the house?"

Patti looked uncomfortable. "Yes."

"And where was that?"

"In her bedroom." Patti's face was flushed.

"And what occasioned your being in Mrs. James' bedroom?"

"She wanted me to help her with her wedding dress. She couldn't find her maid." Patti hastened to add.

"Was this the day of the wedding?"

"No, she was having her portrait done."

"While you were in Mrs. James' bedroom, did you notice anything unusual?"

"I noticed that there didn't seem to be any evidence that she had been married to Roderick Barker, no pictures, no…"

"Objection, irrelevant." Roberta had wondered if Harmon would let that pass.

"Sustained. The jury will disregard the last remark of the witness," the judge instructed.

"Ms. Burleson," Roberta resumed, "did you notice anything else in Mrs. James' bedroom?"

"Yes, while she was showering, I noticed her bedside drawer was open." Patti flushed a bright red. "I know I shouldn't have done it, but I was curious so I looked inside. The drawer was a real mess unlike the outward neatness of the room. I saw a medicine bottle with the name Roderick Barker. I picked it up and looked at it."

"Do you remember what medicine the label stated."

"Digitoxin."

"No further questions, Your Honor," Roberta nodded to Harmon.

Harmon asked all the routine questions of Patti, then after a long pause, he asked. "Ms. Burleson, what did you say was the name of the medicine you saw in Mrs. James' *personal* bedside drawer."

"Digitoxin."

"Is this a medication you use?"

"Objection, irrelevant!"

The judge looked at Harmon. "Where are you going with this Mr. Harmon?"

"The witness' familiarity or lack of familiarity with this medicine bears directly on our defense, Your Honor."

"I'm going to allow it, but get the point, Mr. Harmon," Judge Summerfield admonished.

"Ms. Burleson, is this a medicine you use?"

"No."

"Do you know anyone who uses this medicine?"

"No. Unless you count Roderick Barker."

"If this is not a medicine with which you are familiar, Ms. Burleson, how is it that you remember the name so clearly after two and a half years?"

"Because I wondered why Mrs. James kept it. I thought it might be sleeping pills. I was curious so I asked a friend of mine who is a nurse how it was used. She told me it was a heart medication. I thought it really strange that Mrs. James kept it."

Harmon looked stunned. He hadn't expected this answer. He asked a couple of other questions hoping to discredit her or at least to divert the jurors attention and then sat down.

"State calls Mildred Coleman."

"State your name and occupation for the record, please."

"Mildred Coleman. I am employed as a maid to Mrs. James."

"Ms. Coleman, how long have you worked for Mrs. James."

"I have worked for her since 1989."

"How did you come to be hired by Mrs. James?"

"Oh, she didn't hire me. I worked for Roderick Barker. Mrs. James, she was Mrs. White then, married Mr. Barker, and when Mr. Barker died I stayed on."

"So Mrs. James was married twice before."

"Objection, irrelevant."

"Sustained, jury will disregard. Watch where you're going, Ms. Marshall," the judge warned.

"Where were you on the evening of October 30, 1995?"

"I was in the James' household."

"This is where you work?"
"Yes."
"Do you also live on the premises?"
"I do."
"Where were you when Mr. James arrived home that evening?"
"I was in the entry foyer arranging some flowers."
"Was anyone else present in the foyer?"
"Yes, Mrs. James."
"Can you tell us what transpired between Mr. and Mrs. James?"
"Mrs. James was leaving the house with her purse just as Mr. James was coming in the door. He asked her where she was going. She said she had some errands to run and she would be right back."
"Did either of them say anything else?"
"Mrs. James told Mr. James that she made him a cup of tea and left it by his chair."
"Did Mr. James drink the tea?"
"Not immediately. He opened his mail, then he picked up the tea and drank it all down at once, like he just wanted to be rid of it. He really didn't like herbal tea, you know. He just drank it to please her. She had this thing about herbal flower teas. Thought everyone should drink them. I didn't though. I stuck to my coffee."
"Did you observe Mrs. James make the tea?"
"No, but she told me she was going to make a cup of tea, then she went into the kitchen."
"Did you find that unusual?"
"Yes, she always asks someone else to make her tea."
"Who would she normally ask?"
"Me, the cook, or Mrs. James."
"Mr. James' mother?"
"Yes."
"Did Mrs. James, that is Cynthia James, drink any of the tea?"
"She took a sip and said something about its being weak and tasting bad. She was always trying new blends. I guess she didn't like this one."
"What did she do then?"
"She took a small bottle of sweetener from her pocket and poured it in the tea."
"Did she taste the tea again?"
"No."
"How do you know the bottle contained sweetener?"
"She always carried it. She liked sweet tea and she thinks sugar will kill you."

"Is it possible the bottle could have contained something other than sweetener?"

Mildred frowned, "Yes, I guess that's possible."

"Ms. Coleman, did you ever have an occasion to be in Mrs. James' bedroom?"

"Yes, I clean her bedroom and care for her clothes and personal items."

"Did you ever have occasion to look in her bedside drawer?"

"Yes, I did, a couple of weeks after Mr. Barker's death. I was taking away the remainder of his belongings. She always left her bedside drawer open so I looked in it."

"Can you tell us what you observed in this drawer?"

"A real mess. Drove me crazy. She wouldn't let me straighten it up or throw anything away. I started to throw away Mr. Barker's medicine. She jerked it out of my hand and told me to stay out of her bedside drawer."

"And what was the medicine she wouldn't let you throw away."

"Digitoxin."

"No further questions, Your Honor."

Harmon tried hard to shake Mildred's testimony but the most damaging response he could elicit was that she didn't like Mrs. James. Did she dislike her to the point she would like to help the prosecution?

"No," Mildred said firmly and believably, "I don't lie for anyone."

After a brief recess, Roberta rose, shuffled through her file and announced, "State calls Paul Mitchell."

Roberta had only one question for the EMT who headed the emergency team, which had responded to the 911 call to the James' household on October 30, 1995. "What was Mrs. James' emotional condition?"

"Objection, this witness has not been admitted as an expert in this area."

"Your Honor, EMTs are trained to assess the responses of persons involved in emergency situations," Roberta spoke quickly.

"I'm going to allow it. Overruled. Answer the question, Mr. Mitchell."

"She seemed very cool and collected. She didn't seem upset at all."

As Roberta returned to her seat, Harmon stood up. "Mr. Mitchell, have you had experience with people in shock?"

"Yes, I have."

"Is it possible Mrs. James was in shock?"

"It's possible but not likely."

"But it is possible?"

"Yes, it's possible."

"That's all, Mr. Mitchell."

Roberta took the remaining two EMTs through the same questions. Harmon countered again with the possibility of shock.

Roberta called the insurance agent, Brent Spencer, as her next witness.

"Mr. Spencer, do you know Cynthia James?"

"Yes, I do."

"In what capacity do you know her?"

"She and her husband are...were clients of mine."

"By her husband, do you mean the late Mr. James?"

"Yes, but I was also agent for her and her last husband, Mr. Barker, as well."

"How were Mr. and Mrs. James clients of yours?"

"I sold them each a million dollar life insurance policy."

"Do you mean they each bought a million dollar policy on the other party?"

"Objection, leading the witness."

"Sustained. Rephrase your question, Ms. Marshall."

"Describe the policies which Mr. and Mrs. James purchased."

"Mrs. James purchased a million dollar policy on herself. Mr. James purchased a million dollar policy on himself."

"Who was the beneficiary on Mr. James' policy?"

"Mrs. James."

"Were Mr. James' children secondary beneficiaries?"

"No."

"Did Mr. James have a policy naming his children as beneficiaries?"

"No." Brent gave Cynthia a distressed look. He liked her, and he knew his testimony would not help her.

"Is it unusual for parents not to name their children as beneficiaries?"

"Yes, but Mr. James explained that to me. He said he and Mrs. James agreed that, if anything should happen to him while his children were still in school, she would make sure his children were provided for by using a portion of the money to set up trust funds. He also said he planned to sell his country house and set up portfolios for his children."

Harmon asked Brent when the policies were purchased and made the point that it is not unusual for financially well off people to purchase million dollar policies immediately after marriage. He elicited the fact that two years had lapsed between the purchase of the policies and Mr. James' death.

"State calls Frederick Joseph Franklin."

Roberta knew that Freddie was a less than credible witness, but she felt the other witnesses she planned to call would help make his testimony more believable.

"Mr. Franklin, do you know Cynthia James?"

"Yes, I do."

"Is Mrs. James in the courtroom?"

"Yes, she is."

"Can you point her out, please?"

"She's right there at the defense table."
"How do you know Mrs. James?"
"We grew up down on the riverside and went to school together."
"How well do you know Mrs. James?"
"Very well. We had a thing for a while during high school then she married some old dude."
"Have you had an occasion to see Mrs. James in recent years?"
"Yes, I have."
"When was that?"
"She came to see me at the Riverside Bar back in October of '95."
"Why did Mrs. James come to see you?"
"She wanted me to knock off her husband."

The courtroom erupted into pandemonium. Several reporters rushed to the door. Judge Summerfield banged his gavel loudly. "Order," he shouted, "I will have order in my courtroom." He banged until the roar of voices subsided to a babble. "I will have order in my courtroom, or I will have you all removed. Am I understood?" The absolute silence in the room acknowledged that he had been clearly heard and understood. No one wanted to miss this trial.

"Resume," he said to Roberta with a nod.
"Exactly what did she say to you?"
"She said, 'I want you to kill my husband.'"
"Did you take this statement seriously?"
"She was dead serious," Freddie grinned.
"Did she state her husband's name?"
"She didn't have to. I knew she married that lawyer, Grant James."
"Did she say how she wanted you to do this?"
"Nah, she just said she would pay me two hundred thousand to do it."
"Did you agree to do this?"
"No, I just figured I'd take her money and not do anything. What could she do about it? She ain't going to report me to the police."
"Did she, in fact, pay you?"
"Yeah, she gave me a hundred thousand the next day. Then she gave me a hundred thousand after she knocked off…"
"Objection!!"
"Sustained. Jury will disregard witness' last statement."
"Mrs. James gave you a hundred thousand the second day she met with you, and she gave you another hundred thousand after Mr. James died? Is that correct?"
"Yeah."
"Why did Mrs. James pay you the second hundred thousand if you didn't do anything?"

"She didn't want me to tell anyone she asked me to knock off her old man."
"Have you seen Mrs. James since that time?"
"No."

Harmon stood up with the look of a cheetah stalking his prey. He had a lot to work with here. This was a guy he could discredit. He tried to bring out as much of Freddie's disreputable past as he could.

"Mr. Franklin, did the District Attorney offer you immunity if you implicated Mrs. James?"
"No."
"The DA did not offer immunity from prosecution in this case?"
"No. I didn't do anything to Mr. James."
"Did the DA's office agree to drop any other charges for your testimony?"
"I came forward to do what I thought was right. Being a good citizen, you know."

Harmon thought, "I have to give the sleezebag credit. He's a cool one. His eyes didn't even dart to the prosecutor when I asked that question, but then he didn't answer it either."

"Mr. Franklin, please answer yes or no. Did the district attorney's office offer to drop any other charges?"
"No."
"Did you enter any kind of plea agreement with the district attorney's office?"

Roberta knew Harmon would follow this line of questioning and she knew that Freddie would have to say yes to the plea bargain. She felt, however, that the corroborating witnesses would strengthen his now weakened testimony.

Long pause, "Yes." Freddie knew when he was backed into a corner.
"What was the nature of this plea?"
"Extortion."
"Extortion. Would you please explain."
"I wasn't going to murder her husband. I was just going to take her money."
"What did the DA offer you?"
"Five years suspended for extortion. Without supervision." Freddie smirked.

Roberta still felt she had a good case even though Freddie's testimony was weakened. She would strengthen it with the next witness.

"State calls Officer Paul Crane."

Roberta questioned Officer Crane about his encounter with Cynthia and placed emphasis on his seeing her with Freddie. She next called Cynthia's banker, Bob Tuttle. He confirmed the two withdrawals of a hundred thousand in cash and the dates. He stated he had been concerned that she might be the victim of blackmail, but she had assured him that she was taking a trip and had needed a whole new wardrobe.

Roberta called Jack Reed as her last witness. She first established that Jack was a friend of Grant James and that he was well acquainted with Grant's wife, Cynthia. She then asked him where he had seen Cynthia in October of 1995. Jack was very clear about the date and time that he had seen Cynthia and Freddie together, because he had an appointment with a client and was waiting for his arrival when Cynthia came in. No, he had a feeling she would be embarrassed by his seeing her there in a not so elegant bar. No, she didn't appear to be in any distress or he would have gone to her aid. Yes, he was surprised to see her leave the bar with Freddie, but he just thought she was slumming, maybe having a little fling. No, he didn't find it strange that she had chosen a seedy bar. After all, when she was carrying on an affair with Grant, she had met him at Rose's. Cynthia herself had told Jack about those meetings.

The prosecution's case took the better part of four days. At noon on Friday, the judged recessed for the weekend electing to wait until Monday to allow the defense to begin its presentation. This was exactly what B.P. Harmon wanted. He wanted the jury to have time to forget some of the prosecution's case and to become vague on other parts. He knew Roberta's reputation. She gave one hell of a powerful summation, but then so did he. He loved a worthy opponent. He had to admit, though, he was a little worried. The prosecution had a strong case. His client was really good, however. She almost had him believing she was innocent. He might just put her on the stand.

Harmon chuckled. In all his years of defense work, he had only had one client that he really believed was innocent. He remembered her clearly. A little old woman, wealthy, of course, that's the only kind he defended. She was small, refined, white hair, soft spoken. She was accused of killing her brother. Harmon really believed her and he fought hard to have her acquitted. He had felt really good when he'd been able to walk her out of that courtroom as a free woman. She'd gone home and killed her other brother right in front of his wife.

Monday morning dawned grey and rainy. Cynthia felt depressed. She still couldn't believe that Freddie had turned on her like a rabid dog, after all they had been to each other. B.P. had been encouraging her that they could counter everything that had been said so far. He felt the hardest charge to beat would be solicitation to commit murder. She and Freddie had made no specific plans, so Harmon thought the conspiracy charge wouldn't hold up. He had brought this out on cross-examination of Freddie. She could still hear Freddie's answer. "Nah, I didn't make any plans with her. I didn't intend to do it. I was just going to…" Harmon had stopped him at that point.

Harmon had gone to Cynthia's friends at Veronica's Boutique and bought her a new beige, silk suit that showed just enough leg and neckline to be alluring, but not offensive. He wanted the males on the jury to be distracted by her beauty and vulnerability.

Roberta had been up a large portion of the night. She knew she had to be well prepared because B.P. Harmon was no slouch in the courtroom. She also knew she had to be alert so she forced herself to crawl into bed at three a.m. She was asleep as soon as she lay down.

Roberta felt pretty good as she pulled on her jogging shorts early the next morning. Once around the block and she would have her blood and her adrenaline pumping. She believed that a fifth of a mile in the morning was enough. She usually jogged five miles at night.

"All rise. Court is now in session. Honorable Judge Tom Summerfield presiding."

"Mr. Harmon, are you ready to present your case?"

"I am, Your Honor."

Harmon began by parading a long troop of character witnesses through the courtroom. "Cynthia is delightful."

"Cynthia is very moral."

"Cynthia is responsible," etc., etc., etc. He brought in several expert witnesses as well. Harmon only made one mistake with a character witness. Cynthia's hairdresser was also Roberta's hairdresser. She had commented to Roberta once that Cynthia James really hated her husband. She always said she wished she hadn't married him. Once she had talked about divorcing him. She said she would do it except she wasn't giving him any of her money. Roberta had very carefully elicited this information. The witness seemed to forget she was on the stand and was eager to supply the information to Roberta.

Harmon silently cursed. How could Cynthia have failed to mention those conversations? Harmon had the sinking feeling that he would have no choice but to put Cynthia on the stand. He didn't like putting defendants on the stand. They were generally loose cannons. You couldn't be sure what they would do under pressure. He had thought Cynthia would be a good candidate for the stand, but he wasn't so sure. If she blew off that kind of steam in a beauty shop, Roberta might just be able to bait her into responding when she shouldn't.

"Your Honor, defense requests a brief recess to confer with my client."

Cynthia could see Harmon was furious.

"Why in the hell didn't you tell me you had these conversations with your beautician?"

"I forgot. Besides, I didn't think she would testify about anything but my character. It's the best shop in town. They are usually very discreet."

Harmon heard the last two statements loud and clear. "It's the best shop in town. They are usually very discreet." He suddenly knew as clearly as if he had been told "...the best shop...very discreet." Just the sort of place a young upwardly mobile assistant DA would choose. Roberta knew going in what this woman would say. Harmon cursed himself for not noticing how carefully she worded her questions so as not to trigger an objection. He should have known when she instructed his witness to "tell me only exactly what Mrs. James said to you personally."

~~~~~~~~~~~~~~~~

Cynthia went on the stand early in the day before the jurors were tired while she looked fresh and dewy and vulnerable. She was dressed in a pale blue, raw silk suit, expensive but understated. She wore a simple white blouse with a shirt collar. She looked like every man's beloved younger sister. Her blond hair hung softly around her shoulders framing her face like a halo. Harmon had made arrangements for her to have her hair done. He had the hairdresser lighten it one shade, just enough to shave five years off her appearance.

"State your name and address for the record, please."
"My name is Cynthia James, and I live at 136 Prospect Hill Road."
"Mrs. James, you have heard the testimony in this courtroom regarding Freddie Joseph Franklin, have you not?"
"Yes."
"Do you know Freddie Joseph Franklin?"
"Yes, I do."
"How do you know Mr. Franklin?"
"We have been friends since childhood."
"Do you still regard Mr. Franklin as a friend?"
"I do."
"Why do you think he has told the story about you that we heard earlier?"
"I think someone has forced him to lie about me."
"Who would do that?"
"I don't know."
"Did you have a meeting with Freddie in October of '95?"
"I did."
"What was the purpose of this meeting?"
"I had heard that Freddie's mother was very ill. She was very good to me when I was a young girl."
"So you met him to express concern about his mother, is that correct?"
"Yes, and I thought he might need some financial help. With medical bills, I mean."
"Did you, in fact, give Freddie money to help with his mother's medical expense?"
"I did."

"And how much money did you give him?"
"I gave him one hundred thousand on two occasions."
"A total of two hundred thousand. Is that correct?"
"Yes."
"In what form did you give him this money?"
"What do you mean," Cynthia feigned confusion.
"Did you give it to him by check, money order, or cash?"
"I gave him cash."
"Why would you give him that much in cash?"
"Well, he asked for it in cash. And…I thought my husband was less likely to find out."
"Are you telling us that your husband didn't know you were helping this old friend."
"He didn't know."
"Why didn't you want him to know?"
"He was very jealous. I didn't think he would understand that Freddie was just a friend."
"Mrs. James, you have heard two persons testify that you had a bottle of Digitoxin in your night stand. Is this true?"
"Yes."
"To whom did this medicine belong?"
"My late husband, Roderick Barker."
"Mrs. James, why did you keep this medicine for so long after your husband's death?"
"It…it…" Cynthia faltered and looked about to cry. Harmon smiled inwardly. The little twit was a born actress.
"I know this sounds silly, but it made me feel a little like he was still alive."
"Ms. Coleman testified earlier that you became angry, and I believe her term was 'snatched' it away from her when she wanted to throw it away. Is that true?"
"Yes, I did take it from her."
"Why didn't you tell her why you wanted to keep it?"
"I was embarrassed. I was afraid she would think I was silly keeping a dead man's medicine bottle so I could feel like he was still alive and near."
"The investigating officer who searched your house has testified that he found an empty Digitoxin bottle in your nightstand. Is that true?"
"Yes, he did."
"Was this the same bottle seen by the previous two witnesses?"
"Yes, it was."
"They have testified that the bottle was almost full. What happened to the contents of the bottle?"

"After the incident with Mildred, I decided to throw away the contents and just keep the bottle. Sometimes at night I would just sit and hold it thinking of Roderick."

Harmon was secretly admiring his client unaware that she had just made a fatal miscalculation.

"Mrs. James, did you and your husband purchase life insurance after you were married?"

"We did. We each purchased a million dollar policy."

"Whose idea was it to purchase these policies."

"It was Grant's idea. He had a lot of debts, and he didn't want to risk leaving them for me to pay if anything happened."

"Were you the beneficiary?"

"Yes, Grant felt I would be better qualified to help the children manage than Samantha would or than they would themselves."

Harmon wished she hadn't put down Samantha. First wives always had the sympathy of the jury, especially, if they were the mother of the dead man's children.

"Mrs. James, did you solicit Freddie Joseph Franklin to commit the act of murder upon your husband?"

"I did not." Cynthia didn't look at the jury as she had been instructed.

"Did you conspire with Freddie Joseph Franklin to commit the act of murder upon your husband?"

"No, I did not." Still no eye contact with the jury.

"Damn," Harmon thought, "she's been so good up to now. Doesn't she understand how important it is to make eye contact with the jury when denying a charge."

"Did you kill your husband, Grant James, by administering a lethal dose of Digitoxin?"

Cynthia glanced at the jury a little too quickly to suit Harmon.

"No, I did not."

"No further questions, Your Honor."

"Now, it's up to me," thought Roberta. She had caught a couple of glaring contradictions. She had already thoroughly checked out Freddie. She knew about the sick mother. She also knew that the medical bills had not been paid other than those covered by Medicare. She was prepared to shake that poor, sweet, little widow image Harmon had engineered.

"Mrs. James, can you describe to us what happened on October 30, 1995."

Harmon considered objecting but thought better of it. He didn't want the jury to believe that Cynthia had anything to hide. They had discussed the question of the tea and he felt she could handle it. She was to answer as briefly as possible.

"I had to run an errand so I left briefly before dinner. When I returned and entered the house, I saw Grant on the floor. I rushed over and knelt beside him. His son said they had called 911, because Grant had fallen on the floor and was unconscious. The EMTs came into the room and began resuscitating him. They called him in as a possible heart attack. I started to go with them when his mother stumbled into a table. I guess she had a cocktail and it went to her head…"

Harmon silently cursed. He looked at Margaret James and saw tears well in her eyes. The jury would see that, too. What was it with this woman? Now she was defaming the dead man's mother. She wasn't going to sway any jurors that way. Harmon mentally began planning his appeal.

"I had to leave Mildred to take care of her until her husband arrived. Trey, Grant's son, and I followed the ambulance to the hospital. I wanted to ride in the ambulance but the EMTs suggested that it would be better if I followed. So I drove and Trey rode with me."

"Mrs. James, you stated that you gave Freddie Franklin two hundred thousand dollars to help pay his mother's medical bills. Why did you not pay them directly?"

"I didn't want to offend Freddie by implying I didn't trust him. Besides the more I became involved, the more likely Grant was to find out."

"Are you aware that no money was used to pay any bills? That all payments have been made by Medicare?"

"No," Cynthia feigned surprise.

"Why did you lie to your banker about your reason for needing the money."

Cynthia flushed. "Because it was none of his business," she said a little too sharply.

"Oh, hell," Harmon thought, "she's going to unravel."

"Mrs. James, you testified earlier that your husband made you his beneficiary on his insurance policy, because he had a large amount of debts with which he didn't want to burden you in the event of his death. Is that correct?"

Cynthia looked wary. "I don't remember exactly."

Roberta looked at the court reporter and said, "Could the reporter, please, read back that part of the testimony." After the reporter had dutifully droned out Cynthia's previous testimony, Roberta said, "Now that your memory is refreshed. Is that correct?"

"Yes," reluctantly. It was clear Cynthia had a feeling there was a problem.

"Do you recall the testimony of your insurance agent, Brent Spencer?"

"Not entirely."

"Could the reporter, please, refresh our memory on the Spencer testimony."

After what seemed a very long time, the reporter read the testimony.

"Why do you think your husband did not mention his need to protect you from his debts, and why do you think he said you would provide for his children from the money?"

"He was probably ashamed of his debts. He didn't tell me about them until after...," Cynthia stopped abruptly and her eyes darted to Harmon who was frowning. He realized she had lost her poise. It would be all downhill from here. If she would just fake crying or illness, he could call for a recess and gain time for her to compose herself.

"Has any of the money been distributed to his children since they are still in school?"

"No."

"I believe that in one version of your testimony..."

"Objection, prejudicial."

"Sustained. Rephrase your question Ms. Marshall."

"Mrs. James, you testified earlier that your husband felt you could manage the insurance money better than his children or his former wife, Samantha James. Is that correct?"

"Yes."

"Where is she going with this," Harmon wondered and knew as soon as he asked it.

"Are you aware that Samantha James owns and operates a very..."

"Objection, irrelevant."

"Your Honor, Cynthia James introduced the first Mrs. James into this proceeding by her own testimony."

"I'm going to allow it, Mr. Harmon. Overruled."

Roberta repeated, "Are you aware that Samantha James owns and operates a very successful home decorating business?"

Reluctantly, "Yes, I am."

"In light of this fact," Roberta emphasized fact, "why do you think Mr. James would consider you a better manager?"

Cynthia beamed. She knew how to answer this, "Because in the two years of marriage, I made some very successful and profitable investments."

Harmon looked thunderstruck and Cynthia knew she had given Roberta a weapon.

"Tell us about those investments, Mrs. James."

Cynthia looked frantically at Harmon. He was rapidly writing on his pad. He didn't look at her.

"We're waiting, Mrs. James."

"Objection, badgering the witness." Harmon was trying to break Roberta's momentum. He knew she was walking his client to the gallows, figuratively speaking.

"Overruled." Judge Summerfield gave him a withering look. "I will not have frivolous objections in my courtroom, Mr. Harmon. Maybe you do that in the big city but not down here." He looked at Cynthia James. "Answer the question," he instructed. He knew this went to motive. He knew why Roberta wanted it in and why Harmon wanted to keep it out. Cynthia looked like a scared rabbit. She knew that indulging her ego had trapped her.

"Well, we...that is, I invested in a large tract of land near the intersection of the interstate and Broward Road."

"And what happened with that property?"

"We sold it."

"How much did you sell it for?"

Reluctantly, "Five million."

"Five million," Roberta repeated emphatically. "And what did you pay for that property?"

"Two million."

"Did you pay cash for the property?"

"No, we financed it. Grant couldn't have borrowed the money except for my assets," she hastened to add.

"So on this one investment you made a three million dollar profit in less than two years. Is that correct?"

"Yes," faintly.

"Could you speak up, please, Mrs. James? I'm not sure the jury can hear you."

"Yes," Cynthia repeated sullenly.

Roberta methodically took her through several other successful but less profitable investments.

Samantha hadn't known about these investments. She made a note to talk with Jack. Her children were obviously due a large sum of money even without a formal will. Cynthia's lawyers and accountants had done some fancy footwork that even Jack's thorough investigations had not revealed.

"Mrs. James, your previous testimony indicates you felt very deeply toward your former husband, Mr. Barker, and that you missed him very much, is that correct?"

"Yes, it is," Cynthia was relieved. She felt on firmer ground here, because she had cared for Roderick, although she didn't really miss him now.

"Mr. Barker had a great many beautiful things, did he not?"

"Objection, irrelevant."

The judge raised his eyebrows inquiringly at Roberta.

"The question goes to the issue, Your Honor. I will quickly show the connection."

"Overruled. Answer the question, Mrs. James."

"Yes, he did."

"Were there certain items he cherished more than others?"

"He had a beautiful scrimshaw collection that he really loved. It was quite valuable. He had over one hundred pieces. He never tired of showing them to me," Cynthia reminisced.

"You testified earlier that you kept Mr. Barker's medicine bottle so you could feel close to him. Is that correct?"

Harmon groaned audibly. The judge gave him a sharp warning look. Roberta turned to look at him in surprise, as did everyone in the courtroom. It had worked, however; Cynthia had been warned. Roberta was furious.

"Your Honor, may counsel approach the bench?"

Judge Summerfield motioned them forward.

"Your Honor, he did that deliberately to warn his client of where I was going."

"I'm sorry, Your Honor, my back has been bothering me, and I felt a sharp pain. We haven't had a recess in quite awhile," Harmon complained.

Judge Summerfield looked sour. "I didn't finish the bar yesterday, Mr. Harmon. I know what you are up to and I will not tolerate it. Please resume your cross-examination, Ms. Marshall. There will be no further interruptions," he said looking directly at Harmon.

"Mrs. James, you said you kept Mr. Barker's medicine bottle to feel close to him, is that correct?"

"Yes, but I..."

"Mrs. James," Roberta cut her off, "Mr. Barker had all these beautiful, cherished items, yet you are asking us to believe you kept a prescription bottle of Digitoxin to remember him. Is that correct?"

"Yes," sullenly again. Cynthia silently cursed her stupidity in keeping the bottle.

"Mrs. James, will you remind us of when you disposed of the contents of the bottle?"

"Right after Mildred brought it to my attention by trying to throw away the bottle."

"About how long was that after Mr. Barker's death?"

"Two weeks, I guess."

"Did you have more than one bottle of Digitoxin in the house?"

"No."

"You had one bottle of Digitoxin left after Mr. Barker died. Is that correct?"

"Yes."

"And you disposed of the contents approximately two weeks after his death. Is that correct?"

"Yes."

DEADLY BREW
She Loved Him to Death

Harmon was fully alert. What had he missed? Roberta was carefully taking this somewhere. Suddenly he knew...the other witness...the timing.

"If you disposed of this medicine two weeks after Mr. Barker's death, then how is it, Mrs. James, that Patti Burleson saw a nearly full bottle of Digitoxin in your bedside drawer almost a year and a half later?"

Cynthia realized her error too late. "I don't know," she stammered. "I must have thrown it away after she saw it instead of after Mildred saw it."

"But you didn't know Ms. Burleson saw it, did you, Mrs. James?"

Roberta didn't wait for an answer but went directly to her next line of questioning.

"The evening of Mr. James' death, you made a cup of tea. Previous witnesses have testified you tasted that tea. Is that correct?"

"I did."

"Further testimony says that you took a small bottle from your pocket and poured something into the tea. Is that correct?"

"Sweetener. I put sweetener in it."

"Did you taste it after you poured the liquid into it?" Roberta was careful not to call it sweetener.

"I can't remember." Cynthia was scared and wary now.

"Ms. Coleman testified that you did not taste it afterward, but instead offered it to your husband and left the house, is that correct?"

"Yes," faintly.

"Could you speak up, please, Mrs. James?"

"Yes," sharply.

"Why did you not taste it afterward, Mrs. James?"

"It was a new blend which didn't have a very good flavor. It evidently wasn't pure because it tasted peculiar even though I used the normal amount of leaves. I decided I didn't want it," she shrugged.

"It was so bad you couldn't drink it, but you told your husband you made it for him. Why?"

"I didn't see any point in wasting it," she responded lamely. "Grant didn't know the difference between good tea and bad."

Harmon inwardly groaned. She had put down the first wife, defamed the dead man's mother, and, now, she was belittling the dead man himself. He never should have put her on the stand. He had taken a calculated risk and lost.

Roberta paused for several moments. She turned so she was partially facing the jury.

Harmon knew that move. "Here it comes," he thought. "Be ready."

"I submit to you, Mrs. James, that you did not taste the tea again because you knew it contained the Digitoxin..."

"Objection..."

Roberta rushed on, "because you put it in there from your sweetener bottle."

"...prejudicial, stating a fact not in evidence."

"...is that not correct?"

"Sustained, Ms. Marshall, you're out of line. You pull a stunt like that again, and I'll hold you in contempt." Judge Summerfield scowled. "The jury will disregard the last question."

"I'm sorry, Your Honor, I have no further questions."

"She's good." Harmon thought, "I wonder if she would consider coming over to my firm."

Roberta had planned to recall Freddie Franklin, but she decided that Cynthia's own testimony had been so damaging to the defense's case that she could rest.

Harmon began his summation by pointing to Cynthia and saying, "My client is not guilty. Prosecution has not met the burden of proof. The evidence presented today does not, in fact, prove beyond a reasonable doubt that Cynthia Barker James either intended to murder or did murder her husband, Grant James. Based on the evidence presented here, you can only find her not guilty."

Harmon's impassioned oration pointed out that all the evidence presented had been explained and was non-incriminating. He pleaded that Mrs. Grant James was a distraught and helpless young widow abused and confused by these proceedings. He pointed out that there was no motive. She was already wealthy and didn't need Grant's insurance. He advised that they could only find her not guilty, because there was more than a reasonable doubt about the prosecution's case.

Roberta presented a careful and logical summation of the facts pointing out motive: money, the investments she and Grant had shared had been hidden and not distributed to his children; the insurance on which she had been the sole beneficiary, none of which had been distributed to his children. She pointed out opportunity: the cup of tea, which she offered to a trusting and unsuspecting husband. She emphasized means: the Digitoxin from her former husband. The State had presented evidence that showed conclusively that Cynthia Barker James did solicit a hitman to murder her husband, conspired with this hitman to accomplish the act and finally did, herself, premeditate, and poison her husband thereby depriving him of his life.

~~~~~~~~~~~~~~~~

The jury retired to deliberate after having received instructions from Judge Summerfield on proper conduct and on which charges they could find Cynthia guilty or not guilty: solicitation of a person to commit the act of murder; conspiracy to commit the act of murder; and murder in the first degree.

Sarah Carlton was quickly chosen as the foreperson, just as Roberta had predicted. Sarah had already decided that she was going to whip this jury into shape and have a verdict out of it in no time flat.

"I think the first thing we should review are the possible charges," she began. "These are the six findings we can make: guilty of solicitation of the act of murder; not guilty of solicitation of the act of murder; guilty of conspiracy to commit the act of murder; not guilty of conspiracy to commit the act of murder; guilty of murder in the first degree; or not guilty of murder in the first degree."

"I think we should discuss each charge individually. I suggest we begin with solicitation first, because if we conclude she didn't solicit then its unlikely she conspired. Therefore, we can quickly dispose of that charge. The first degree murder charge should be discussed last, since the evidence is less clear and it will require more discussion."

She hesitated briefly to make a couple notes then without waiting for comments from the others, she continued. She arose and began writing on the blackboard.

"According to my recollection evidence which points to solicitation is as follows.

1. Freddie Joseph Franklin testified that she asked him to kill her husband and paid him two hundred thousand dollars to do it.
2. There were two corroborating witnesses, Jack Reed and Officer Paul Crane who saw them together just prior to the death.
3. Cynthia Barker James admitted that she gave Freddie Joseph Franklin two hundred thousand but said it was for medical bills.
4. Bob Tuttle confirms that she withdrew one hundred thousand dollars on two different occasions in October of 1995."

"Is there any discussion on this matter?" she looked around the room.

Barbara Walker, one of the middle class jurors, asked, "Isn't it possible that she really did give him the money to pay his mother's medical bills?"

One of the male, blue-collar jurors snorted and said, "You must be joking. Rich broads that look like that don't pay medical bills for the mothers of sleezebags like Freddie Franklin!"

Barbara flushed and looked offended but didn't say anything else.

Margaret Dalton, the black grandmother, spoke, "Remember that she wasn't always rich. She grew up down on the riverside."

A man in the back spoke up, "You know, this guy is a previously convicted felon. I wouldn't put it past him to tell her his mother had to have some expensive medical procedure. Everyone knows how expensive doctors and hospitals are. I might believe that. He could have just done that and then spent the money on something else."

"Amen," said Margaret Dalton. She remembered her own mother suffering because they didn't have the money for some much needed surgery.

"Why didn't she tell her banker?" another of the middle class ladies questioned.

"It seems strange to me that she felt a need to lie to him."

"She said she didn't want her husband to know."

"I doubt if her banker would have called him up," the woman commented.

"I still say she ain't paying no medical bills for no poor old lady. She cheated her husband's kids, didn't she?" No one responded.

"Any other comments or questions?" Sarah asked. No one spoke up. "Let's take a vote then. All in favor of a guilty verdict on the solicitation of the act of murder charge, raise your right hand." Eleven hands went up immediately. Barbara Walker slowly raised hers to make it unanimous.

"Good," Sarah said as she efficiently checked off the first charge and wrote guilty beside it. "We've disposed of one charge. Let's move on to the next one."

"On the charge of conspiracy to commit the act of murder. I recall the following evidence:

1. Cynthia James did meet Freddie Franklin and ask him to murder her husband.
2. Freddie Franklin says they made no plans because he had no intention of doing it at all.
3. Cynthia James denies ever even discussing it.
4. There are no other witnesses to their conversation."

"Discussion, please."

"If she asked him to do it. I'd say that's a form of planning," someone spoke in the back of the room.

"As far as I can tell they never did anything further together in order to make this happen. I believe that you have to do something toward making this happen."

"She paid him the money and he accepted it."

One of the blue-collar workers stood up, "I've read extensively on the law. I planned to be a lawyer as a kid, but I didn't have the money for law school," he explained. "You have to have a lot more than one meeting to convict on conspiracy. Let's face it; they met. He says she ask him to murder her husband. She says he asked for money for his mother. We've no way of telling who is lying here, but someone is. He says they made no plans. She denies the whole thing, so really all we have is the meeting or two meetings and the money."

After a long silence, Sarah asked for further discussion. When there was none, she called for a vote.

Two of the middle class jurors raised their hands to vote guilty. Ten including Sarah, voted not guilty. Sarah thought Cynthia was as guilty as soot is black, but she also felt there was virtually no evidence on this count. She pointed this out to the two guilt-sayers. After extensive discussion, the two women admitted there was clearly reasonable doubt that the conspiracy charge had been proven.

Sarah carefully checked off the conspiracy charge, then marked it "not guilty." She looked at her watch. It was seven o'clock. The bailiff would be coming to take them to dinner in a few minutes. She suggested that they begin deliberations on the murder charge the following day when they were fresh, since it would likely be a lengthy session. All agreed and the request was sent to the judge. He dismissed them for the day.

~~~~~~~~~~~~~~~~~

The jurors filed into the jury room. None of them looked rested. It was obvious that most of them hadn't slept well. Sarah thought, "It's no wonder. Deciding someone else's fate doesn't lie easy on the mind." Sarah was a no nonsense, let's get the job done sort of person, but she had not slept well wrestling with this problem.

"Shall we begin?" She queried. Eleven heads nodded.

"On the charge of murder in the first degree, she must have had motive, opportunity, and premeditation. The evidence as I see it is as follows."

Sarah walked to the blackboard and began to write on one side.

Motive-Pro
1. Hated him-told her hairdresser.
2. Insurance money-sole beneficiary.
3. Successful investments after marriage-hidden from children during probate.

"Help me with evidence to motive," Sarah requested. "Either on the pro-side or the con-side."

"Well, you can hate your husband and still not kill him," one woman suggested and then blushed.

"I don't think the insurance was a motive with all her other money," a timid young man stated.

"If it wasn't a motive, why didn't she give some of it to his kids as she promised, and what about that five million dollars she kept for herself? How come she didn't give some of that to his kids?"

"Three million," another voice said, "only three million was profit."

Sarah was impatient. "How many think the money was a motive?"

More than half the hands went up. Sarah put a big plus beside each of the two money listings.

"How many think she hated him enough to kill him?"

Only a couple of hands went up. Sarah put a big minus by the hate listing.

After three hours of discussion, there was unanimous agreement that Cynthia clearly had motive, and that the motive was money.

Sarah was pleased with herself. She was running a tight ship here. This jury was not wasting any time on frivolous conversation.

"We now need to determine if she had the means and opportunity to commit this murder," she said.

Returning to the board she began to list what she saw as evidence. After a couple of hours and considerable debating, the evidence list was complete.

1. Two persons had seen the full Digitoxin bottle in her bedside drawer.
2. She had lied or been confused about when she disposed of the contents.
3. They were all in agreement that she had wanted her husband dead, and had taken steps to make that happen. They based this on Freddie's testimony, which they believed, although they were divided on why he came forward, and on the testimony of the hairdresser.
4. She had added something to her tea, which she did not taste or drink afterward, but gave it to her husband. They were all in agreement that, if it tasted so bad she couldn't drink it, it was unlikely she would offer it to anyone else.
5. She left the house so that she would not be present when the heart attack occurred.

Some of the jurors pointed out that it was not clear as to what errand she was on at the time. Several felt there was no errand, she just wanted to be out of the house.

Finally, Sarah brought up the final point, premeditation. There no longer seemed to be a question about whether she solicited Freddie. There was a great deal of heated discussion about why Cynthia would hire Freddie and then do it herself. Margaret Dalton spoke up, "Sometimes you have to take opportunities when they present themselves, because you just know other people can't be depended upon."

"How did she know he was going to be coming in as she was leaving," someone asked. There was pretty general agreement that she more than likely knew when he was due, because they were expecting guests, and the chance that she heard his car drive up was very good.

No one believed she had kept the bottle of medicine to remember Roderick. That didn't make sense. Why not keep one of the scrimshaw pieces or the whole collection for that matter. She didn't need the money. One of the middle class women had reminded them that Patti Burleson had been struck by the fact that Cynthia had evidently gotten rid of all of Roderick's belongings "as if he had never lived there."

They all had been impacted by the testimony of the EMT's that she was very calm and efficient in handling the situation, showing no emotional upset. The defense had argued shock and had put Roderick's doctor on to show that she was calm and efficient during the time of his death. The prosecution had pointed out that Roderick's death came slowly over a long period of time, and she'd had time to prepare herself.

Harmon cursed when the call came to say the jury was in. They had deliberated less than fourteen hours over the two-day period. That couldn't be good for his client. He couldn't say he hadn't expected it, however. He berated himself for putting Cynthia on the stand. She had hung herself.

~ ~ ~ ~ ~ ~ ~ ~ ~ ~ ~ ~ ~ ~ ~ ~

The prosecution, defense, and news people hurried into the courtroom. Samantha and Forest were already there. Margaret and Grant's children filed in soon after.

Judge Summerfield asked the jury if they had reached a verdict.

"We have, Your Honor." Sarah passed the verdict sheet to the bailiff who handed it to the judge. Samantha watched the judge's face. He gave no sign. He just read the paper and passed it back to the bailiff.

"Will the defendant, please, rise," he instructed.

Cynthia stood, wringing her hands. She was somberly dressed today in a black Dior suit, which while expensive and well cut, did nothing to lift the mood at the defense table. Harmon was stoic.

Roberta felt optimistic. A short deliberation probably favored the State's case but, of course, one could never be sure.

The judge looked to the jury. "Madame Foreman, how do you find on the charge of solicitation to commit the act of murder?"

"Guilty as charged."

"How do you find on the charge of conspiracy to commit the act of murder?"

"Not guilty."

Roberta was stunned. She had not expected this given the evidence. "How could you find her guilty of solicitation and not of conspiracy?" Roberta wondered. Harmon felt encouraged.

Even the judge seemed surprised. He hesitated momentarily then continued. "How do you find on the charge of murder in the first degree?"

"Guilty as charged, Your Honor."

Cynthia sank into her chair sobbing. Harmon began quickly assuring her that they would appeal.

Roberta turned to look at the James family. Samantha was hugging her children. Margaret James was silently sobbing into her hands. Forest James rose and stuck his hand out to Roberta. "Thank you," he said simply and turned to console his wife.

Sentencing was set for the following Monday, and Cynthia was led away to begin her frightening new life.

Chapter 29

It was a beautiful day, clear blue sky, a soft breeze, and mild temperature. The picnic spot offered a panoramic view of the lake glittering like a bowl of diamonds in the sunlight. Soft ripples created an intricate pattern with a dazzling effect. Sailboats drifted lazily in and out of view. Happy couples, enjoying the perfect early June weather, laughed gaily. Delighted shrieks of children's laughter filled the air. Peter and Samantha stood mesmerized by the surroundings. A feeling of peace and contentment emanated from them. Words were not necessary. They had planned this picnic on several occasions, but had postponed it because of so many unexpected events in Samantha's life. The wait had been worth it. They shared a companionable silence. Both were lost in their own thoughts embraced by the sense of serenity. Neither could remember experiencing such tranquility before. Unconsciously, they moved closer together, each needing to touch. Peter slid his arm around her waist. Samantha rested her head upon his chest feeling his gentle energy caress her. A contented sigh escaped her lips. Silently, she wondered why she had ever considered resisting such a loving presence. Intuitively, Peter felt her surrender and knew their relationship had shifted to more solid ground. His arm instinctively tightened around her. He never wanted to let her go. He had waited all his life for this deep, unspoken, mature love. He wanted to share everything with her…spring flowers bursting through the ground to salute a new day, the smell of fresh air after a summer rain, the brilliant colors of autumn leaves, a walk in the woods after a fresh snow. He wanted to share every sensation, every emotion with her.

Peter wanted to keep the day carefree and gay in the hope that Samantha would relax. He had appealed to the boy in himself and purchased a beautiful kite that was safely tucked away in the trunk of his car.

"Wait here, right here," he said grinning sheepishly as he loped off to the car. Samantha stared after him wondering what he was up to. She had observed the mischievous glimmer in his eyes. She gasped with delight when he came into sight carrying the most beautiful kite she had ever seen. Jumping to her feet she raced to meet him already anticipating the adventure.

"Oh, Peter, it's beautiful. What a wonderful surprise! I love kites. I haven't flown one since Trey was a little boy, and never one this magnificent."

Peter beamed, "I knew you'd like it. I could hardly keep from calling you last night to tell you all about it, but that would have ruined the surprise."

Peter was proud of his selection. He had spent hours making his decision and had stayed up very late last night to assemble his treasure. It barely fit in the trunk of his car. A beautiful butterfly with wings of gold and black spanning almost five feet. Its body was an iridescent blue with antennae bouncing in the breeze. It was so realistic that he expected it to flutter its wings and disappear in search of a flower garden.

Peter was thrilled by Samantha's reaction. "Before we launch it, we've got to name it," he said.

Samantha laughed softly, "Well, it is obvious. We'll call her 'Madame Butterfly'."

Her excited chatter was music to his ears. She began to reminisce of wonderful afternoons with Trey at the park with his kite. The memories brought a warm glow to her face and a twinkle to her eyes. Breathlessly, they launched their 'Madame Butterfly' and watched it gracefully climb higher and higher. A magnificent sight with outstretched arms embracing the universe. Peter was so happy he wanted to do the same thing. His spirits were soaring for he realized he was in love with this vibrant woman beside him. He felt as high as the kite. From Samantha's flushed glow, he concluded she shared his feelings to some extent.

"Oh, Peter, I haven't had so much fun in ages. It was great to do this with Trey, but it feels so special with you. It is fun, laughing and playing with you. I feel like a teenager."

Peter and Samantha frolicked like children keeping their beautiful butterfly airborne. The shouts and cheers from the sightseers in the passing boats exhilarated them. They were having so much fun that they had forgotten their picnic, until their stomachs growled in protest. Reluctantly, Peter began pulling the kite while Samantha spread a red and white checkered tablecloth on the boulder overlooking the lake. She began unpacking the treats that Betsy, Peter's housekeeper, had prepared. Samantha's mouth watered as the basket revealed french bread, brie, pate, hard salami, fresh fruit, and a very good bottle of Chardonnay complete with crystal glasses. Somehow she felt the crystal wineglasses had been Peter's touch. She had him pegged as a true romantic.

Peter's eyes widened when he saw the spread that Betsy had sent. "Goodness, I hope you're hungry. Betsy must have thought we'd be gone awhile."

"Isn't it great. I'm starving, so maybe Betsy knew best. You must give her my compliments."

The sun was setting as they relaxed against a huge oak tree, sipping their second glass of wine, physically spent from their frolicking, but emotionally charged. It had been a day of awakening for both of them. Samantha felt Peter's gaze and turned, her eyes staring at the long legs stretched casually on the cool earth, moving the length of his body to slowly meet his eyes. Her breath caught by what she saw there, such tenderness and longing. She sat motionless, hypnotized by the unspoken depth of feeling and her unbidden response.

Peter reached for her hand and brought it to his lips. With no more than a whisper, he said, "Samantha, I feel so much. I don't want to rush you or frighten you away, but I can't remain silent. I love you. I want you for all time. I feel so many emotions. Desire, oh, yes, but it is much more than that. I've searched for you my entire life. You're everything I ever dreamed of, hoped for. You complete me. Please tell me you feel something for me."

Samantha's throat tightened. She was so overwhelmed, words would not form. Peter's words echoed her thoughts. He touched her soul and stole her heart. Pure unconditional love consumed her. Tears of joy threatened. Without a word she was in his arms. He held her tightly, placing soft kisses in her hair, on her forehead, and finally on her lips, slowly, tenderly, tasting and savoring the delicious nectar of her response. Pleasure deepened with each caress stoking the fire until the heat seared their souls...soulmates united by their intense need.

The sun had long since disappeared, and stars were blinking their approval, when Peter and Samantha loaded the kite and picnic basket and headed home. A comfortable silence embraced them as they watched the lights of the city grow larger. They had spent the evening answering all the questions the other had longed to ask. Peter had shared his tragic loss of Amy, his first wife, and Samantha had poured out her hurt and anger at Grant's betrayal. She told of the pain and the joy of motherhood. Peter was looking forward to meeting her children. He had always wanted a family; maybe he would have one at last.

~~~~~~~~~~~~~~~~

Samantha heard the phone ringing as she inserted the key in the door. Letting Peter find his way to the den, she dashed for the phone. She answered breathlessly. "Hello. Yes, this is Samantha James...Officer Brooks?...What is wrong?"

Peter whirled as he heard her sob, "Oh, no. It can't be true." He was at her side in three quick strides holding her closely, while she clutched the phone sobbing. Realizing she was distraught, he took the phone. His frown deepened as the officer explained the purpose of the call. Forest and Margaret James had been in an automobile accident. Forest had swerved trying to avoid falling debris from a truck, then he lost control of the car and went over an embankment. He was pronounced dead at the scene. Margaret, unconscious, was enroute to Memorial Hospital. Peter advised the officer he would drive Samantha there. Peter held Samantha a few minutes before gently leading her to the door.

She pulled away abruptly, "I've got to call the children. Oh God, how do I tell them?" Covering her face with her hands, she moaned, "They just lost their father and now a grandfather and maybe a grandmother."

She started to tremble, her knees buckled, but for Peter, she would have crumpled to the floor. Peter pulled her close and took her hands from her face and turned her toward him.

"Samantha, I'm so sorry. I'll help you through this. Why don't we check on Mrs. James' condition and then call them? I have my cell phone. Where are the children?"

Samantha allowed him to guide her to the car. "Trey is at a sports training camp in Atlanta, and Sadie is attending a summer session at Wooster."

As he helped her into the car, he said. "As soon as we get to the hospital, I'll call the airlines and make all the arrangements." Driving toward the hospital, Peter wished he could spare her this pain, but he knew that all he could do was to be there and lend her support. Samantha closed her eyes and thanked God for sending her Peter. She knew she would need his strength to get through this. Trey and Sadie would be devastated. She had to be strong for them. They had lost so much in their young lives.

Upon their arrival at the emergency room, they found the news was not optimistic. Margaret James had not regained consciousness. She had severe head trauma and numerous other internal injuries. It would be hours before anything was known. Disheartened, Samantha placed calls to Trey and Sadie. Her call to Sadie tore at her heart. Sadie was so close to her grandparents. She wrote to them frequently and loved spending time with them when she was home. Her sobs were agonizing for Samantha. She wished she could be there to take Sadie in her arms and to console her and give her strength. Samantha felt so helpless. Her call to Trey was even more traumatic. He sobbed and begged his mother to say it wasn't true. He shouted that he wouldn't let God take them. Samantha's comforting words seemed not to help. She had to do something to calm him. He was so angry at the unfairness of it. She understood his feelings. He had lost his dad, now a grandfather, and possibly his grandmother, who was holding on by a thread.

"Trey, I can't explain it or justify it, but your father and grandfather had strong beliefs. They trusted in God and asked for His help in time of need. I think that is what we need to do. We all need to ask for guidance. Honey, tonight ask for strength and guidance. Your prayers will be heard. Will you do that for me?"

Trey replied in a hoarse whisper, "I'll try, Mom, I'll really try."

Samantha hated not being with him. If only she could hug him and ease the pain. Dropping her head in silent prayer, she asked God to allow them to see their grandmother one last time.

After several hours, Dr.Sims suggested Peter take her home for awhile. They would call her if Margaret's situation changed.

Chapter 30

Samantha had taken only enough time to shower and change before returning to the hospital. She couldn't take the chance of not being there if Margaret regained consciousness. Samantha closed the door softly behind her. Margaret looked so frail lying there attached to all those tubes. Samantha could hardly believe this was the strong, healthy woman she had seen on Friday morning. She studied Margaret's face. There was no evidence of life, no twitching, no eye movements. Only the beeping of the life support units reassured Samantha that Margaret was indeed still alive.

"Mother, it's Samantha, I'm here. Please, don't leave, Mother. I need you here. The children need you." For a moment Samantha thought she saw the eyelids flicker. It was most likely her imagination, she realized. The doctors had said Margaret was in a coma. After awhile Samantha drifted off to sleep, her head resting in her arms on the side of the bed.

"Wake up, Samantha, wake up." Samantha opened her eyes to see Grant standing across the bed from her. He said, "Wake up, Samantha, it's important you wake up."

"But I am awake," she protested.

"You must wake up now, Samantha." He kept insisting. Samantha was a little irritated. Why couldn't he see that she was awake?

Samantha shook her head groggily. She raised up looking for Grant. She realized she had been dreaming. Then she heard it again. Someone whispered her name. She jerked around. Margaret's eyes were open and her mouth was moving. Samantha moved closer. "Yes, Mother, I'm here."

"You must tell them," Margaret whispered.

"Tell who, Mother, the children?" Samantha asked.

"You must tell them," Margaret repeated. "It was I."

"What was you, Mother? I don't understand. Were you driving the car?" Samantha was bewildered. What was Margaret trying to tell her?

"Grant...tell them it was I." Margaret was evidently delirious.

"It's Samantha, Mother, not Grant."

Margaret was becoming agitated. "Samantha, it was I...Grant. I didn't mean to do it...not to my Grant. It was wrong, but I wanted her out of his life."

Samantha realized that Margaret was trying to tell her something she had done to Grant. "It's all right, Mother; I'm sure Grant understands," Samantha tried to console her mother-in-law.

"No, no, you don't understand. Cynthia didn't do it. I did. You must tell them. She shouldn't be in prison for something I did. You have to tell them."

Samantha's mind felt frozen. She couldn't be hearing what she thought she was hearing. "Mother, you're confused. Cynthia is in prison because she murdered Grant."

"She didn't do it. I did." Margaret whispered.

"Mother, what are you saying, are you saying you caused Grant's heart attack?" Margaret's eyes had closed again.

"Oh, please, Mother, you can't go now," Samantha cried. "Oh, please, wake up. I have to know."

Margaret's eyes fluttered. She looked at Samantha. Her eyes glazed and then cleared. She seemed to be making a tremendous effort to focus and speak.

"The tea...for Cynthia...not Grant," she said.

"What tea?" Samantha was completely confused.

"Day of heart attack..." Margaret's voiced trailed off.

"Oh, please, God, don't take her now," Samantha could see Margaret was struggling to stay conscious.

"Found Dad's medicine that day...put in my pocket. She was...Grant so...unhappy. The tea was just sitting there...thought she made if for herself...not...Grant."

Realization began to dawn on Samantha. "You put the digitalis in Cynthia's tea, but Grant drank it instead?"

Samantha felt ice cold. This could not be happening. She was having a nightmare. Of course! She had seen Grant telling her to wake up. She was still asleep.

"Samantha," Margaret was barely whispering. "So sorry. You must tell them...let Cynthia go. Please...forgive me." Margaret's strength was gone. Her eyes closed. Samantha's attempts to rouse her were to no avail.

Samantha dropped her face into her hands and sobbed audibly. This was more than unbearable. This was unspeakable. How could she ever tell anyone? "It wasn't fair of Margaret to make this my burden," Samantha thought miserably. Samantha reached for the nurse's call button. The duty nurse appeared promptly.

"She was conscious briefly," Samantha said. The nurse quickly checked Margaret who showed no indication of consciousness.

"Sometimes they open their eyes but that does not mean they are conscious," she said.

"No, she spoke to me," Samantha said. The nurse looked startled, "She spoke to you, what did she say?"

"She just called my name," Samantha said a little too quickly. The nurse stepped to the EEG machine and checked the printout. "This shows several minutes of beta activity," she sounded surprised. She stepped to the intercom and requested a page for Dr. Sims. The nurse smiled at Samantha. "This is a good sign."

Samantha stared at her blankly. "A good sign," she repeated. Her mind did not comprehend.

~~~~~~~~~~~~~~~

Cynthia tugged at the ugly, orange jumpsuit. It was routine county issue, stiff and scratchy. Tears formed in her eyes. It wasn't fair. She hadn't poisoned Grant. She didn't understand how Freddie could have done it either. She certainly didn't understand why he would turn on her, if he had. He pleaded that he never planned to follow through. He just planned to take her money. They gave him immunity. She had paid him well. "And for nothing," she thought. "But if Freddie didn't do it, who did?" The county medical examiner had said that digitalis worked within thirty minutes.

Cynthia reached back mentally to that day. Who had been there? "Trey...no." Trey and his dad had regular disagreements, but they were not serious, and Trey really loved his dad. "Mildred...no." Mildred was genuinely fond of Grant. Cynthia was also aware that Mildred disliked her. "Maybe Mildred did it to set me up. Oh, Cynthia, get a grip, you're getting paranoid," she thought. Mildred was too timid and not nearly smart enough for that. "Margaret..." Cynthia laughed ruefully and dismissed that thought. Margaret James doted on her precious son; she'd never do him in.

Cynthia suddenly felt weak. "The digitalis was in the tea. I left the tea in the kitchen while I answered the phone. Margaret was in the kitchen." Cynthia suddenly remembered the peculiar taste. She also recalled how Margaret had reacted when she broke the empty teacup. "Oh, no! Oh, no! Not my Grant, not my Grant."

"She intended to kill me. Guard, guard, I have to call my lawyer," she called frantically.

"You've had your call for the day. You'll have to wait until tomorrow."

Cynthia began crying. She was feeling defeat and elation at the same time. All she needed was for Margaret to admit she poisoned the tea.

After awhile Cynthia turned on the television. Her lawyer had fought for this privilege. The newscaster was droning on. Cynthia half listened until she saw Forest's face on the screen. "Forest James, owner of James Fine Furniture Company, was killed in an automobile crash earlier this evening, while trying to avoid debris falling from a truck. His wife, Margaret James, was in the vehicle with him. She is in Memorial Hospital ICU. Mrs. James is in a coma. An unidentified source at the hospital said her condition is grave. Her family are at her bedside."

Cynthia felt the blackness closing in on her.

Chapter 31

It was not yet dawn, but Samantha was pacing the floor. She was still at the hospital. She feared if she left, Margaret might awaken and want to talk again. She was still in a state of shock by what Margaret had revealed to her. Her shoulders slumped with the heavy burden of it. She refused to think about it right now. Her children needed her undivided attention. They both had early morning flights. She had brought her makeup and toothbrush, so she could freshen up before meeting their flights. She did not want to be late. She dreaded telling them that their grandmother was still unconscious. "God, please, give them strength to accept this disaster without leaving them crippled emotionally."

~~~~~~~~~~~~~~~~

Samantha headed for the terminal gate. Sadie's flight arrived first. Samantha had been glad of that, because Sadie was very mature and could help console Trey. What a sad homecoming for them both. Peter had offered to come with her, but she felt it would make the children uncomfortable. She would tell them about him at a happier time.

Sadie's flight was being announced just as Samantha arrived at the gate. She didn't have long to wait since Peter had insisted on first class seats for both children. Sadie caught sight of her instantly and ran to her.

"How is Grandmother?"

Samantha sadly shook her head. "Not good, she awoke last night for a few minutes and then lapsed into unconsciousness again. It doesn't look encouraging."

Sadie collapsed in her arms and wept. Samantha hugged her tightly and murmured her sorrow. After regaining her composure, Sadie whispered, "I love them so much. I'll miss Grandfather terribly. I can't give up Grandmother, too. They are all we have left of Dad. Why, Mom? I just don't understand."

"I know, baby, I've asked the same questions. We just need to pray that God will help us find a way to accept it. We still have each other. We need to hurry to meet Trey's flight. He's still not recovered from your father's death. He'll need all the love and support we can give him."

Trey's arrival brought more tears and comforting words from both Sadie and Samantha. Trey hugged his mother. "Mom, are you all right. I was so upset last night. I'm so sorry I yelled at you. I know you love Grandpa and Grandma James, too."

"Oh, Trey, it's okay. I know you weren't angry with me. You don't need to apologize. I just felt so helpless because I couldn't make the pain go away." Samantha smiled sadly as she brushed his hair off his forehead.

They were bound by a common grief. Only Samantha knew there was more. With linked arms Trey, Sadie, and Samantha moved out of the terminal strengthened by their unity. The final farewells that lay ahead of them did not seem quite so frightening as before.

When they arrived at the hospital, Dr. Sims advised them that it was doubtful Margaret James would make it through the next few hours. He felt sure she would not regain consciousness. He did allow Sadie and Trey a few minutes alone with their grandmother. Sadie would later insist that her grandmother smiled when she heard their voices. Through the evening, they sat huddled on a couch with Samantha, waiting for the inevitable. It was late afternoon when they were jarred out of their daze with the announcement system calling a "Code Blue." Nurses and technicians rushed to their grandmother's bedside. Samantha put her arms around her children. They knew their grandmother was gone and they wept. With heavy hearts they stood waiting for the official word, then emotionally spent, they left the hospital. Samantha drove them home knowing that now she needed to make double funeral arrangements.

Hours after the children were in bed, Samantha sat clenching and unclenching her hands. She stared into space recalling Margaret's last words to her. It was an ironic twist of fate. Poor Margaret, how had she lived with her secret? At first Samantha had felt anger for a wasted life, but she knew it had been an accident. "Could you really call it an accident? Was there such a thing as an accidental murder?"

She no longer felt anger, only a void existed. A void that only time would heal. What would she tell the children? She didn't want to tarnish the image of their beloved grandmother. How would they react to this dark secret after losing both their grandparents? How could she destroy their precious memories?

"Oh, God, why did this have to happen? Dear God above," she prayed, "You give me strength to do what is right."

Samantha's thoughts turned to Cynthia. "She is an evil woman who hired a hitman to take Grant out. She deserves to be in prison," Samantha rationalized. "She destroyed my life. Worst of all she caused deep and lasting pain to my whole family."

She thought of the pain and torment Margaret must have endured. Samantha struggled with her conscience. What price should Cynthia pay for the deliberate hurt she inflicted?

"If she has a chance she will go after another married man," Samantha thought bitterly. "Her kind never change." How could Samantha let her have that chance again? She didn't just leave one victim, she wreaked serial damage to whole families. She left a trail of broken hearts and pain. Children were her innocent victims left with shattered values, tarnished heroes, and broken dreams.

"She has no remorse for her actions. She is guilty of multiple crimes," Samantha raged. "She should be punished." Samantha was torn, she could feel no compassion for Cynthia; but it had been Margaret's last wish that this wrong be righted, and she knew that was why Grant had come to her in a dream. Samantha wished she had never heard the confession. She'd just like to forget it all.

"Could I? Forget it? Just pretend Margaret never awakened?"

Moving across the room she picked up a picture of Grant, Trey, Sadie, and herself. They had been a good family and had many fond memories to sustain them. She stared at the smiling faces and knew with gut wrenching certainty that, regardless of the decision she made, lives would be irrevocably changed. Either way she would have to live with the bitter consequences. Samantha decided she would have to carry her extra burden until time and circumstances helped her make the right decision. Who should endure further pain, Cynthia or two innocent children? With a heavy sigh, Samantha turned out the lights, and went slowly upstairs where she knew another restless night awaited her.

Hours later Samantha jerked awake; she was tense and wet with sweat. The dream had been haunting, no terrifying. Samantha untangled herself from the sheets and slowly sat up. She replayed the dream in slow motion, feeling her chest and throat tighten. It was even more disturbing to her now that she was awake. With great effort she pulled herself up, changed into a dry gown, and crawled back in bed. She was physically exhausted and emotionally drained. She barely had he strength to pull the comforter over her. She knew what she must do. It was the only answer. Maybe now she could sleep. With her decision made, she closed her eyes to seek the comfort of peaceful, dreamless sleep.

Chapter 32

Samantha shook her head groggily. She had slept like the dead last night and now she wasn't waking up easily. She had made a decision last night after the dream. Samantha re-ran the dream in her mind like a movie.

She was walking down a path through a great forest. Everything was twilight. She felt small and frightened. Abruptly, the path divided. Down one path she could see her children. They were small again and her heart filled with love and the desire to protect. Down the other path a gray stone building towered menacingly over a small black casket resting on the pathway. Samantha quickly started down the path toward her children. She felt a sense of urgency as she rushed toward her small children. She must protect them from the evil in that building.

Suddenly, she saw Grant and Margaret. They were smiling. She felt safe and happy. As she approached, they turned their backs and began to walk away. Now she saw her parents. She took her children's hands and ran toward them. They were not smiling. Her father turned and walked away. Her mother lingered a moment. Her mouth didn't move but Samantha heard her say,

"You know you have made your bed,
"To live a life with truth unsaid,
"To live a life that is untrue,
"Well, daughter dear, that's a deadly brew."

Samantha's mother was no longer there. She turned to see her children, but they were adults now. They no longer needed her protection.

Samantha had awakened to a feeling of darkness and heaviness. She had thought about the dream for a long time before she realized the message.

Samantha didn't want to face this day. Slipping her feet into the big fuzzy slippers Trey had given her, she began to slip-slap her way to the kitchen. She knew a good cup of coffee would clear her head and prime her for the task ahead.

Her cheerful kitchen usually lifted her spirits. This morning she hardly noticed where she was. Even the aroma of coffee brewing failed to help. She poured a cup of coffee and sipped for a few minutes before returning to her bedroom to prepare for the ordeal ahead. Samantha donned a conservative blue pantsuit. She didn't feel like being noticed today.

Despite everything, Samantha did feel somewhat relieved as she backed the car from the driveway. She no longer needed to feel resentful of Margaret for putting her in this position. She had prayed for guidance and had received it. She drove quickly to the police station. She had decided to handle this through

Sgt. Martin. He would know the proper procedure. Besides, she felt comfortable with him.

Samantha swung into a parking space, shut off the engine, and closed her eyes. She needed to take a few slow, deep breaths to prepare for the distasteful task ahead.

Every fiber of her being screamed, "Justice was done." She knew it had not been. She had already delayed longer than she should have.

Samantha opened the door and began the ten feet walk to the front desk. Everything was moving in slow motion. She had to consciously concentrate on placing one foot before the other. The pretty female officer at the desk was watching her. From some vast region of space she heard a voice asking for Sgt. Martin.

"He's pretty busy right now. Can I help you?"

Samantha's voice rose with anxiety, "No, I have to see Sgt. Martin."

The officer looked at her curiously. She could hear the panic. "Why do you need to see him?"

"It's about the James murder. I have some information."

The officer looked shocked but was instantly alert. "I'll tell him your are here. What's your name?"

"Samantha...Samantha James."

The officer disappeared around the corner. In less than a minute Sgt. Martin was at Samantha's side.

"What is it, Samantha? You're white as a sheet. Let's go to my office so you can sit down."

He looked at the officer. "Myra, bring her some water."

After Samantha was seated with a glass of water, she regained her composure; although Sgt. Martin could see she was still tense.

"Now, Samantha, what's this all about? What information do you have?"

"She didn't do it?" Samantha's voice trembled.

"Who didn't do what?" Sgt. Martin queried gently.

"Cynthia. She didn't do it."

Sgt. Martin was puzzled. How could Samantha know? He had only heard a few minutes ago.

"How do you know this, Samantha?"

"She told me just before she died." Samantha was sobbing now.

Sgt. Martin was confused. How could she have told Samantha before she died. Had Samantha had some sort of psychic experience or was she having a breakdown.

"Start at the beginning, Samantha. Tell me how you know this."

Samantha blew her nose loudly. This was so out of character that her state of mind impacted sharply on Sgt. Martin.

"Just before she died, she whispered it to me."

"How could she whisper it to you?" Sgt. Martin was speaking softly and soothingly. He liked this woman and hated seeing her distraught. He would have liked nothing better than to comfort her and send her home, but it was his job to find out what she knew or thought she knew.

"I was there. She called my name and whispered it to me."

Sgt. Martin was startled and more convinced than ever that Samantha was having a breakdown. "You were there! In the prison?" He spoke louder than he intended.

Samantha looked at him bewildered. "In the prison? You said prison instead of hospital."

Sgt. Martin was thoroughly confused now. "Hospital?" He spoke quietly again. "She was never in the hospital, Samantha. She died in prison. Who told you about this?"

Samantha was alert now. "Who died in prison?" A feeling of dread swept over her. She realized that he must be talking about Cynthia. He had no way of knowing about Margaret.

Sgt. Martin frowned. If Samantha didn't know about Cynthia, what was she trying to tell him? "Samantha, Cynthia James was murdered some time last night. We don't know who did it yet. They slit her throat, then put the knife in her hand to try to make it look like a suicide."

The small black casket in the dream flashed into Samantha's consciousness. She began sobbing again. Deep wrenching sobs of guilt.

Sgt. Martin didn't understand. Samantha was very satisfied when Cynthia was sentenced to prison for killing her husband. Why was she so upset over Cynthia's murder unless...He shook the idea from his mind. Samantha wasn't that kind of woman. He did need to pursue this further, however. Why was Samantha so sure Cynthia had not killed herself.

"Samantha, what information do you have about Cynthia's death? Why are you so sure she didn't kill herself."

Samantha was inclined not to tell him the true reason she was there. Why expose her children to that grief now that Cynthia was dead. She quickly realized that if she didn't tell him she could appear to have knowledge of who killed Cynthia. She personally had motive to want her dead. Samantha winced to think of how many times she had wished Cynthia dead but never this way. No, there was no turning back now.

Still, if she had only waited another day, she wouldn't have to tell. Samantha's conscience pinched. She had delayed and a woman was dead. She had to at least clear Cynthia's name. She had promised Margaret...and in a way, Grant, too.

"Oh, Bob," Samantha had never called him by his first name before. He was pleased. This little gesture said she trusted him. "I'm not talking about Cynthia's death. I didn't even know. I'm talking about Grant's death. She didn't kill him."

Sgt. Martin groaned inwardly. What a mess! He felt his heart squeeze. Samantha was on the verge of telling him something he didn't want to hear. He didn't want to have to put this gentle, sweet woman in handcuffs and book her for a murder, which had already put one woman in prison and brought about her death.

"Samantha, I think you had better have an attorney present before you say anything further."

Samantha flinched as though she were dodging a blow. "Are you going to charge me with obstructing justice?"

Sgt. Martin was confused again. He definitely felt he had missed some vital point in this conversation. "Obstructing justice? In what way?" Sgt. Martin was visibly relieved but was at a loss to know how she might have obstructed justice.

"Samantha, you had better start at the beginning and tell me the whole story."

Sgt. Martin reached to turn on his tape recorder, thought better of it and dropped his hand on his desk.

Samantha's voice was barely audible. "Margaret, Grant's mother, told me just before she died that Cynthia didn't kill Grant," Samantha paused for a long time.

Sgt. Martin forced himself to sit silently, waiting. Finally, Samantha spoke again, "Margaret did it."

Sgt. Martin couldn't help himself. He almost shouted, "She poisoned her own son?"

Samantha trembled. She could see that he was as shocked and horrified as she had been.

She spoke slowly, numbly, "She didn't mean to do it. It was an accident."

"How can you accidentally put Digitoxin in someone's tea?" he demanded.

Samantha hated having to do this. A feeling of resentment toward Margaret washed over her again. "She did it on impulse. Cynthia made the tea for herself. Margaret apparently put the Digitoxin in it from Forest's, Grant's father's, medicine bottle. She didn't want to kill anyone. She just wanted to make Cynthia suffer a little for all the pain she was causing others." Margaret hadn't said that to her. She just thought it made it seem a little less terrible. She continued, "The rest you know. Cynthia didn't like the tea and gave it to Grant."

Sadly, she added, "He drank it and died. She loved him so much. She wanted to save him from that...that..." Samantha couldn't say it now that Cynthia was dead. Dead because Samantha had waited too long to tell.

"She loved him to death," Sgt. Martin said tiredly. "What a tangled mess people make of their lives in the name of love," he thought.

Aloud, Sgt. Martin said gently, "Go home, Samantha, forget everything about this terrible tragedy. They are all beyond our help now. I can't bring myself to cause your children any further grief by revealing this. It would serve no purpose. Cynthia's family are all dead, so no one will be grieving over the loss of her good name. Go home, put it all behind you and get on with your life."

Samantha gave him a grateful look. Impulsively, she hugged him. "You are a good man, Bob Martin. Thank you for sparing my children any more pain."

Sgt. Martin watched as she walked away. He wished he could spare her also, but he knew she would carry a heavy burden for a long time.

THE END

ABOUT THE AUTHOR

T. F. Sisters holds several advanced degrees and has traveled extensively throughout the world. It is from these travels and years of experience in law, psychology, medicine, corporate management and everyday life that the plot for *Deadly Brew*, a first work of fiction, was developed. Sisters, who was born in southeastern Oklahoma and spent the early years there with family, presently commutes between Tennessee and Oklahoma, and is currently completing a second mystery.

www.ingramcontent.com/pod-product-compliance
Lightning Source LLC
Chambersburg PA
CBHW030756180526
45163CB00003B/1045